CONTENTS

APPENDICES 70

THE PONY CLUB PRINCE PHILIP CUP OBJECTIVES

The Prince Philip Cup provides a team competition requiring courage, determination and all-round riding ability on the part of the team members, with careful and systematic training of their ponies.

The objective is to encourage a higher standard of riding throughout The Pony Club and to stimulate among the future generation a greater interest in riding as a sport and as a recreation.

This competition was designed for teams of ordinary children on ordinary ponies and the practice by some Branches of retaining their own ponies to be used by successive Members of the Branch/Centre Team was certainly not envisaged by those who devised the Mounted Games concept. The Mounted Games Committee does not approve of this practice.

Where "Branch" is stated this includes "Centres". All competitions are open to Branches and Centres. When a rule states District Commissioner, Centre Proprietor also applies.

Members are expected to abide by the following principles:

"As a Member of The Pony Club, I stand for the best in sportsmanship as well as in horsemanship.

I shall compete for the enjoyment of the game well played and take winning or losing in my stride, remembering that without good manners and good temper, sport loses its cause for being. I shall at all times treat my horse with due consideration."

RULES

These Rules are made by the Pony Club Mounted Games Committee in conjunction with other Pony Club Committees.

The Pony Club Office provides administrative support. Queries relating to these rules should be directed to the Mounted Games Chairman at mgchairman@pcuk.org and copied to the Office at mountedgames@pcuk.org.

Every eventuality cannot be provided for in these Rules. In any unforeseen or exceptional circumstances or any other issue in connection with Pony Club Mounted Games it is the duty of the relevant officials to make a decision in a sporting spirit and to approach as nearly as possible the intention of these Rules.

THE PONY CLUB MOUNTED GAMES COMMITTEE

Chairman

▸ Ian Mariner - mgchairman@pcuk.org

Committee Members

▸ Alison Bell
▸ Marcus Capel
▸ Tracey Cooksley
▸ Pernle Drummond
▸ Vicki Dungait
▸ Marian Harding
▸ Carol Howsam
▸ Brian Ross
▸ Catriona Willison
▸ Andrew James (Area Representative)
▸ Fran Rowlatt-McCormick (Area Representative)
▸ Caroline Barbour (Co-opted Regional & Youth Representation)

Sports Development Officer - mountedgames@pcuk.org

Area Coordinators:

▸ Area 1 - TBC
▸ Area 2 - TBC
▸ Area 3 - TBC
▸ Area 4 - Elaine Barker
▸ Area 5 - Clare Dawson
▸ Area 6 - TBC
▸ Area 7 - Caroline Chadwick
▸ Area 8 - Simon Duddy
▸ Area 9 - Caroline Queen
▸ Area 10 - Alison Davies
▸ Area 11 - Sheila Barbour
▸ Area 12 - TBC
▸ Area 13 - TBC
▸ Area 14 - Nicola Way
▸ Area 15 - TBC
▸ Area 16 - TBC
▸ Area 17 - Biffy Booth
▸ Area 18 - Dennis Whitney
▸ Area 19 - May Wylie

Thank you to all our Volunteers, Area Coordinators, and especially the Committee, for their hard work and commitment over The Pony Club year.

Area Coordinator is a voluntary role with the aim of giving as many Pony Club members as possible the opportunity to try the sport of Mounted Games. An Area MG Coordinator must be passionate about Mounted Games and knowledgeable about its rules. They should be over the age of 21 and have experience of being a team trainer, team manager, line steward, MG Committee member or DC. They can be an existing or previous member.

The Pony Club
Lowlands Equestrian Centre, Old Warwick Road, Warwick, CV35 7AX
Telephone: 02476 698300
pcuk.org

Health and Safety: safety@pcuk.org

NOTE: Rules which differ from those of 2023 appear in bold type and side-lined (as this note). Rules which require extra emphasis will also be in bold.

PART 1 - GENERAL RULES OF MOUNTED GAMES

1.   DRESS

New equipment is not expected, but what is worn must be clean, neat, tidy and safe. It is the competitor's responsibility to ensure their dress complies with the Rules below which does not allow for the wearing of coloured silks and pom poms, brightly coloured accessories, nail polish and jewellery or sponsor advertising.

Hat silks are to be dark blue, black or brown in nature and must not have a logo larger than 4cm x 4cm. Contravention may incur disqualification.

Hats and white hat bands: The last rider in each team to go must wear a white hat band 5cm wide round their hat. They must be wearing the white hat band **at the start of the race** and throughout the race and failure to do so will incur elimination.

a)   Hats and Hair:

Hair: Must be tied back securely, in a safe manner to reduce the risk of hair being caught and to prevent scalp injuries.

Hats: Members must always wear a protective hat when mounted. Only hats to the following specifications are acceptable at any Pony Club activity. The Pony Club is consistent with fellow BEF (British Equestrian) Member bodies in its Standards for Riding Hats. Individual sports may have additional requirements with regard to colour and type. It is strongly recommended that secondhand hats are not purchased.

The hat standards accepted as of 1st January 2024 are detailed in the table below:

Hat Standard	Safety Mark
Snell E2016 & 2021 with the official Snell label and number	
PAS 015: 2011 with BSI Kitemark or Inspec IC Mark	

(BS) EN 1384:2023 with BSI Kitemark or Inspec IC Mark	
VG1 with BSI Kitemark or Inspec IC Mark	
ASTM-F1163 2015 & 2023 with the SEI mark	
AS/NZS 3838, 2006 with SAI Global Mark	

Note: Some hats are dual-badged with different standards. If a hat contains at least one compliant hat standard it is deemed suitable to competition, even if it is additionally labelled with an older standard.

- For cross-country riding **(at all levels)** including Eventing, Arena Eventing, Tetrathlon and Hunter Trials, together with Pony Racing (whether it be tests, rallies, competition or training) and Mounted Games competitions, a jockey skull cap must be worn with no fixed peak, peak type extensions or noticeable protuberances above the eyes or to the front, and should have an even round or elliptical shape with a smooth or slightly abrasive surface, having no peak or peak type extensions. Noticeable protuberances above the eyes or to the front not greater than 5mm, smooth and rounded in nature are permitted. A removable hat cover with a light flexible peak may be used if required.

- No recording device is permitted (e.g. hat cameras) as they may have a negative effect on the performance of the hat in the event of a fall.

- The fit of the hat and the adjustment of the harness are as crucial as the quality. Members are advised to try several makes to find the best fit. The hat should not move on the head when the head is tipped forward. The Pony Club recommends you visit a qualified BETA (British Equestrian Trade Association) fitter.

- Hats must be replaced after a severe impact as subsequent protection will be significantly reduced. Hats deteriorate with age and should be replaced after three to five years depending upon the amount of use.

- Hats must be worn at all times (including at prize-giving) when mounted with a chinstrap fastened and adjusted so as to prevent movement of the hat in the event of a fall.

- For Show Jumping: hat covers, if applicable, shall be dark blue, black or brown only. Branch/Centre team colours are permitted for team competitions.

- For Dressage: hats and hat covers must be predominately black, navy blue or a conservative dark colour that matches the rider's jacket for Area competitions or above. The Pony Club Hat silk is also acceptable.

- For Mounted Games: hat covers, if applicable, shall be dark blue, black or brown only.

- The Official Steward / Organiser may, at their discretion, eliminate a competitor riding in the area of the competition without a hat or with the chinstrap unfastened or with a hat that does not comply with these standards.

Hat Checks and Tagging

The Pony Club and its Branches and Centres will appoint Officials, who are familiar with The Pony Club hat rule, to carry out hat checks and tag each hat that complies with the requirements set out in the hat rule with an Pony Club hat tag. Hats fitted with a Pony Club, British Eventing (BE) or British Riding Club (BRC) hat tag will not need to be checked on subsequent occasions. However, the Pony Club reserves the right to randomly spot check any hat regardless of whether it is already tagged.

Tagging is an external verification of the internal label and indicates that a hat meets the accepted standards. The tag does NOT imply any check of the fit and condition of the hat has been undertaken. It is considered to be the responsibility of the Member's parent(s) / guardian(s) to ensure that their hat complies with the required standards and is tagged before they go to any Pony Club event. Also, they are responsible for ensuring that the manufacturer's guidelines with regard to fit and replacement are followed.

For further information on hat standards, testing and fitting, please refer to the British Equestrian Trade Association (BETA) website: British Equestrian Trade Association - Safety and your head (beta-uk.org)

b)   Body Protectors:

A body protectors is compulsory for **all** Pony Club Cross Country riding (including Arena Eventing) and Pony Racing activities whether it be training or competition. A body protector for these activities must meet BETA 2018 Level 3 Standard (blue and black label).

For general use, the responsibility for choosing body protectors and the decision as to their use must rest with Members and their parents. It is recommended that a rider's body protector should not be more than 2% of their body weight. When worn, body protectors must fit correctly, be comfortable and must not restrict movement. BETA recommends body protectors are replaced at least every three to five years, after which the impact absorption properties of the foam may have started to decline.

Air Jackets

If a rider chooses to wear an air jacket in Cross country or Pony Racing, it must only be used in addition with a normal body protector which meets BETA 2018 Level 3 standard (blue and black label). Parents and Members must be aware that riders may be permitted to continue after a fall in both competitions and training rides for Cross Country and / or Pony Racing if the First Aid provider has no concerns about their welfare. In the event of a fall, an air jacket must be fully deflated or removed before continuing, the conventional body protector must continue to be worn. Air jackets must not be worn under a jacket. Number bibs should be fitted over the air jacket loosely or with elasticised fastenings.

c)   Jodhpurs/Riding Tights: For National Trials, RWHS and HOYS riders must wear cream or beige jodhpurs or riding tights. At all other levels legwear must be black, beige or cream, and there must be uniformity across the team, including the 6th member. There must be no thigh sized logos or brand names, white or other coloured jodhpurs/ riding tights are not allowed. Belts may be worn.

d)   Shirts: White shirts with long sleeves (which are not to be rolled up) and Pony Club ties. In cold or wet weather white sweatshirts and/or colourless transparent or white waterproof garments with long sleeves may be worn over the white shirt. At Area Meetings teams will wear their Branch/ Centre coloured bibs over their shirts or sweatshirts. Bibs may be provided for teams competing at Zone Finals and the National Championships if there is a clash of colours.

e)   Footwear: Only standard riding or jodhpur boots with a well-defined square cut heel may be worn. Plain black or brown half chaps may be worn with jodhpur boots of the same colour. Tassels and fringes are not allowed. No other footwear will be permitted, including wellington boots, yard boots, country boots, "muckers" or trainers. Boots with interlocking treads are not permitted, nor are the boots or treads individually.

Stirrups should be of the correct size to suit the rider's boots (see the Stirrup rule). Laces on boots must be taped for Mounted Games only.

f) **Badges:** These are optional. If worn, they should be of cloth, not metal, and may be sewn on to the bib.

g) **Jewellery:** the wearing of any sort of jewellery when handling or riding a horse/pony is not recommended and if done at any Pony Club activity, is done at the risk of the member/their parent/guardian. However, to stop any risk of injury, necklaces and bracelets (other than medical bracelets) must be removed, as must larger and more pendulous pieces of jewellery (including those attached to piercings) which create a risk of injury to the body part through which they are secured.

h) **Whips and spurs:** are not allowed.

i) **Electronic Devices:** (i.e. headphones, mobile phones etc. enabling another person to communicate with the rider) are not allowed whilst the rider is competing. No recording device is permitted. (e.g. head/bridle cameras etc.)

j) **Acrylics/gels and other false nails are not allowed.**

k) **Sponsor Advertising:** is not allowed on rider's dress, numnahs and saddlery unless they have been presented at The Pony Club Championships in the current or previous years.

2.   SADDLERY

The Pony Club prefers competitors to use plain saddlery but it is not compulsory. New equipment is not expected, but what is worn must be clean, neat and tidy and safe.

Any misuse of a bit or bridle will be reported to the District Commissioner / Centre Proprietor, Area Representative and the Training Chairman. Any reported riders will be recorded, monitored or maybe disqualified.

Badly fitting or unsafe tack, or saddles that are down on the withers when the rider is mounted, will result in the disqualification of that competitor, unless they decide to re- present in the correct saddlery/equipment to the satisfaction of the Official Steward, before the start of the competition.

No item of tack may be used for any other purpose, or in any other way than the one for which it was designed and intended, e.g. Running Martingales may not be used as Standing Martingales.

Saddlery which is not allowed in the Games may not be worn on the day of competition. Any Team/Individual found to have changed, or altered the fitting of, an item of Tack/Clothing, without permission, may be penalised by disqualification from the competition.

The Official Steward has absolute discretion in ruling on these matters.

a) **Saddles:** Must be made on a conventional general-purpose tree Racing saddles measuring less than 16 inches (40.6cm) in length (i.e. from front arch to cantle) and weighing less than 5lb (2.8kg) are NOT permitted. The use of Pad Saddles is only permitted on small native type ponies, with the written permission of the DC and the agreement of the Official Steward. Where handles cannot be removed, these must be taped up. If the stirrup bars have safety clips, they must be in a downward position.

b) **Stirrups:** Stirrups should be of the correct size to suit the rider's boots. They must have 7mm (¼") clearance on either side of the boot. To find this measurement, tack checkers should move the foot across to one side of the stirrup, with the widest part of the foot on the tread. From the side of the boot to the edge of the stirrup should not be less than 14mm.

There are now many types of stirrups marketed as 'safety stirrups'. All riders must ensure that their stirrups are suitable for the type of footwear they are wearing and the activities in which they are taking part and that the stirrup leathers are in good condition.

There are no prescribed weight limits on metal stirrups, however with the advent of stirrups of other materials, weight limits are frequently given by manufacturers. Any person buying these stirrups, should comply with weight limits defined on the box or attached information leaflets. Neither the feet nor the stirrup leathers or irons, may be attached to the girth, nor the feet attached to the stirrup irons.

It is strongly recommended that the design of the stirrup chosen allows the foot to be released easily in the event of a rider fall. Specific rules for individual sports can be found in the respective sports rulebooks.

Particular focus should be on ensuring that the boot and stirrup are the correct size for the rider taking part and used in line with the manufacturer's guidance.

For the avoidance of doubt, at Pony Club events:

- ► stirrups which connect the boot and the stirrup magnetically are not allowed
- ► Interlocking boot soles and stirrup treads are not allowed

Bostock & Free Jump stirrups are not allowed at Pony Club Mounted Games events.

Stirrups which include metal/metal type treads, including but not limited to those with protruding spikes and / or perforated grip features are NOT permitted.

c)   **Girths:** White, navy blue, brown or black girths with two separate buckles. Humane girths are not allowed. Humane girths pose an increased risk as many common designs may have complete girth failure if a single strap was to break. Humane girths are not permitted in any Sport, whether during training or competition.

d)   **Numnahs / Saddle Cloths:** Any solid colour is permitted. Contrasting piping is permitted. Branch/Centre logos are allowed when competing for the Branch/Centre; logos must not exceed 200 sq. cm. This does not preclude the wearing of clothing for horses or riders that has been presented by sponsors of the National Championships in the current or previous years.

e)   **Bridles:** Plain black or brown leather. Micklem bridles are permitted (with rings taped). Bitless bridles are not allowed.

f)   **Reins:** For safety reasons, knotted reins must be attached to the bit by a leather buckle or billet. Large loops of rein behind the knot are not safe, this can be avoided by undoing the buckle or by taping the looped reins together. Any plain solid-coloured reins are permitted for Mounted Games.

Bridge/Market Harborough/Balance Support reins are not permitted.

g)   **Grass Reins:** (Allowed for Junior and **Novice Junior** competitions only)

Only those grass reins shown in diagrams 1 and 2 are permitted. Grass reins must be fitted to allow and not restrict the normal head position of the pony. The rein length must be sufficient to allow the pony to stretch over a small fence.

Grass reins may be leather or synthetic material, if synthetic then a break point of leather or other suitable material must be included

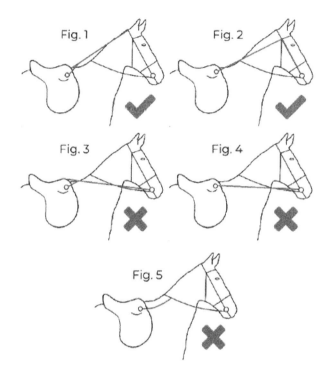

h) **Browbands:** coloured are permitted.

i) **Nosebands:** Only one noseband is permitted – Cavesson, Drop, Grackle or Flash unless using a Standing martingale with a drop or grackle noseband in which case the addition of a cavesson is allowed. Nosebands must not incorporate chain or rope.

Note: Sheepskin nosebands/,blinkers or any attachments to the pony or bridle which may affect the animal's field of vision are NOT permitted.

j) **Martingales:** Irish, Bib, Running, Standing (with or without elastic), only one of which may be worn at any time. Standing Martingales may be attached only to a Cavesson Noseband or the Cavesson portion of a 'Flash' noseband fitted above the bit. Five-point breast plates are allowed.

Vaulting, balance, neck straps/collars are NOT permitted.

k) **Bandages/Boots:** Should only be worn where necessary and not for decoration. They must be of uniform colour and correctly fitted.

l)   **Hoof Boots:** are not allowed.

m)   **Studs:** The use of Studs is not recommended unless absolutely necessary. If worn, road studs may be used. In adverse weather conditions the studs illustrated below may be used.

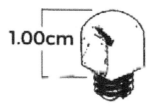
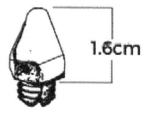

n)   **Fly hoods, ear plugs and ear covers:** Are NOT permitted

o)   **Nose nets are permitted:** Nose nets must cover the nose only leaving the mouth and bit visible.

p)   **Clips on saddlery:** are not permitted.

q)   **Bits:** The bit must be a plain snaffle with a straight bar, single or double joint in the middle. The mouthpiece must be smooth all round. Bits of nylon or other synthetic material are permitted, should be black, brown or white and must be used in their manufactured condition without any addition to/or on any part. Bit Guards must be black, white or brown and smooth on both sides.

Thin Bits – In the opinion of the Chief Steward and the Tack Officials, bits deemed to be excessively thin in the mouthpiece will not be accepted.

Hanging Snaffle bits must be of a standard type. Dr Bristol and Fulmer bits are not allowed.

The only bits permitted for use at Area level and above are those illustrated below or any combination of the mouthpieces, rings or cheeks.

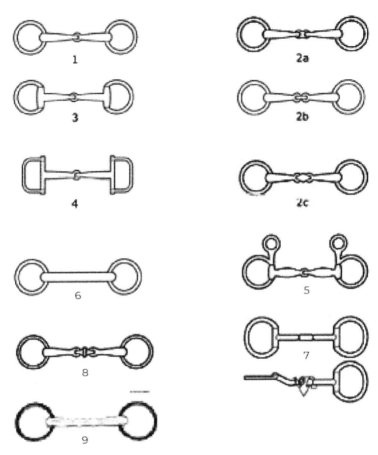

- ▸ 1. Loose ring snaffle
- ▸ 2.a Snaffle with double-jointed mouthpiece (French link)
- ▸ 2.b Snaffle with double-jointed mouthpiece
- ▸ 2.c Snaffle with double-jointed mouthpiece with Lozenge
- ▸ 3. Egg-butt snaffle
- ▸ 4. Racing snaffle D-ring
- ▸ 5. Hanging cheek snaffle (standard type only)
- ▸ 6. Straight bar snaffle. Permitted also with Mullen mouth and egg butt rings.
- ▸ 7. Snaffle with rotating mouthpiece
- ▸ 8. Snaffle with rotating middle piece
- ▸ 9. Un-jointed wavy snaffle (plastic or rubber only)

3. PONIES AND VACCINATIONS

Must be serviceably sound and well shod, or with their feet properly dressed.

Ponies must be groomed and well trimmed, and manes and tails must not be plaited. Ponies that are infirm through old age, ill, thin or lame or are a danger to their riders or others are unacceptable. Veterinary letters regarding the soundness/condition of a pony will NOT be accepted.

At Area Competitions and Zone Finals a pony may compete in the PPC, Novice Juniors, Juniors and Pairs if in the opinion of the DC/Centre Proprietor and the owner that the pony is fit enough and used in the appropriate number of races

Any pony that becomes distressed may be withdrawn from the competition at the discretion of the Official Steward.

THE PONY CLUB VACCINATION RULES

A valid passport and vaccination record:

- ▸ must accompany the horse/pony to all events
- ▸ must be available for inspection by the event officials
- ▸ must be produced on request at any other time during the event

All ponies/horses must be compliant with the current Pony Club minimum vaccination requirements - please see the website for the current rule.

Note: Events that are held at other venues may be subject to additional specific rules. For example, any horse/pony entering a Licensed Racecourse Property must comply with the Vaccination requirements as set by the British Horseracing Authority. Similar restrictions apply in the cases of certain polo venues. If you are intending to compete under FEI Rules you will need to ensure you are compliant with those Rules.

4. ACTION AFTER A FALL

As a training organisation we wish riders to be able to continue whenever possible. However, a rider must not be allowed to remount after a fall if there is any element of doubt as to their fitness, irrespective of the wishes of their parents, trainer, etc. Further participation may be possible following an examination by a medical professional.

a) Any competitor who has a serious fall or injury anywhere at the competition site MUST see the medical personnel on the day and be passed fit to ride before riding that horse in a further test or before riding any other horse.

b) If a rider appears seriously injured (e.g. unconscious) the Official Steward has the discretion to stop the race. They will do this by blowing his whistle and all Line Stewards will raise their boards in response. When a race is stopped through injury it will be re-run; the team involved or the team of the fallen rider may not re-run. Any team that has completed the race prior to the incident will retain their final placing. Any team who has not completed will re-run.

5. HEAD INJURY AND CONCUSSION

There are strict procedures around the response to concussion.

a) General Advice

Head injuries and concussion can be life changing and fatal. Serious head injuries are usually obvious, but concussion can be very subtle. It may not be immediately apparent but should be taken very seriously.

Members may be asked not to ride by an Official (including a first aider) who believes they may have sustained a concussion either at the time of injury or from a previous injury (which may not have been sustained whilst riding). Concussion is difficult to diagnose, and practitioners of all grades must err on the side of caution. Thus, any decision must be respected, and professional medical support is advised to avoid further harm. Ignoring an official's advice about concussion would breach the Pony Club's Code of Conduct.

b) Accidents that could cause head injuries or concussion

Any Member who suffers an incident that could cause head injury or concussion at a Pony Club activity (for example, a fall from their horse/pony) should be assessed by the first aid provider in attendance.

Dependent on the level of first aid cover, the exact process of diagnosing will vary depending/based on whether the Member has suffered:

▶ No head injury/concussion
▶ Suspected head injury/concussion
▶ Confirmed head injury/concussion

The process for diagnosing each option is talked through in more detail below.

From the assessment being carried out it may be immediately obvious that there is no cause for concern. Reasonable care should be taken to ensure

Members have not sustained a serious head injury or concussion.

c) Unconsciousness

If a Member is unconscious following an incident they should be treated as if they are suffering with a confirmed concussion and the steps in point vii should be followed.

d) Who can diagnose head injury or concussion?

Diagnosis of a head injury or concussion can be carried out by Trained First Aiders, Qualified First Aiders or Medical Professionals officiating at a Pony Club activity. If there is any doubt as to the diagnosis, the Member should see the highest level of first aid cover that is present, and they should make the diagnosis. If unable to reach a definite diagnosis or the first aider is the highest level of cover at the activity, then the Member should be referred to a hospital or a doctor off site for a professional diagnosis.

The member must not ride again until they have been seen by a doctor/hospital.

e) Actions to be taken in the event of a suspected head injury or suspected concussion diagnosis

If a diagnosis of a suspected head injury or concussion is made by a first aider, the parents/guardians should be advised to take the member to hospital.

Any Member who has been diagnosed with a suspected or confirmed head injury/concussion should not be left alone and must be returned to the care of their parents/guardians where appropriate.

If a Member has a suspected head injury/concussion at an activity/competition, organisers should inform the DC/Proprietor to ensure that the rider follows these guidelines.

Once a diagnosis of suspected head injury or concussion is made by the first aid cover present at the activity, then that decision is final. If a Member is advised to see a doctor because of suspected head injury/concussion and the parents/guardians decide not to allow the member to be examined (either at the activity or in hospital), the Member will not be allowed to ride again on the day and should be treated as if they have sustained a confirmed head injury/concussion. Depending on the circumstances, the decision not to allow further examination may be considered a safeguarding issue.

Where a doctor subsequently certifies that a Member does not have or did not suffer a head injury/concussion, and provides evidence that they are satisfied the Member is well enough to continue, that Member will be treated as if they did not sustain a concussion and may continue. Officials will endeavour to assess members in a timely way; however, head injuries can evolve over time, which may lead an official or professional to perform a series of assessments. A Member may miss a phase or part of an event during the assessment process and the Sport Rules for missing that phase or part will apply.

f) Actions to be taken in the event of a confirmed head injury or confirmed concussion

In the event of a confirmed head injury or confirmed concussion diagnosis, the doctor will advise the Member not to ride or take part in any activity that potentially involves hard contact for three weeks. The member may be advised that they could request a review of any ongoing concussion problems by a doctor (with experience in assessing concussion) after 10 days. If that doctor is happy to certify that the Member is not suffering with a concussion, the Member may ride again. Evidence regarding this decision is required, e.g. in the form of a medical letter. If no evidence is provided, the Member should not take part in any Pony Club activity that involves horses/ponies, whether mounted or unmounted, for at least three weeks after the initial injury.

g) Actions to be taken in the event of a diagnosis of a confirmed or suspected head injuries/concussions outside of Pony Club activities

Ultimately, it is the parents/guardian's responsibility to make a decision about the welfare of their child.

If a Pony Club Official becomes aware that a member has sustained a suspected or confirmed head injury/concussion and has been advised not to take part in any potentially hard contact activities, the Member must not be allowed to take part in any Pony Club activities that involves horses/ponies, whether mounted or unmounted for three weeks, unless appropriate medical evidence of fitness to ride can be provided by parents/guardians dated at least 10 days after the initial injury.

Please see Appendix 11 for the Head Injury and Concussion Flowchart.

6.   MEDICAL SUSPENSION

If a Member has been suspended from taking part in any activity/competition/sport for medical reasons, this suspension must apply to all Pony Club activities until such time the Member is passed fit by a medical professional to take part. It is the Member and parent/guardian's responsibility to ensure this rule is adhered to.

Medical letters are required, following a suspension for medical reasons, to allow a Member to take part in any activity again. The letter should be issued by the either the hospital or specialist(s) involved in treating the injury, where appropriate.

7.   UNSEEMLY BEHAVIOUR

Unseemly behaviour on the part of riders, team officials, or team supporters will be reported as soon as possible by the Official to The Pony Club Office, and they may be penalised by disqualification of the Branch/Centre or Branches/Centres concerned for a period up to three years. Any competitor who in the opinion of the Official Steward, or Organiser, has been extremely rude or aggressive towards any officials at a competition or who has behaved in an aggressive or unfair manner to their horse may be disqualified.

8.   PERFORMANCE-ENHANCING DRUGS

All performance-enhancing drugs are strictly forbidden and The Pony Club supports 100% clean sport.

a) Equine – Controlled Medication

It is essential for the welfare of a horse/pony that appropriate veterinary treatment is given if and when required. Some medication, however, may mask an underlying health problem so horses and ponies should not take part in training or competition when taking such medication and any Therapeutic Use Exemptions (TUE) should be confirmed in writing by a Vet.

b) Human

Performance-enhancing drugs are forbidden. The Pony Club supports the approach taken by the UK Anti-Doping Agency in providing clean sport. The Pony Club disciplinary procedures would be used in cases where doping may be suspected including reporting to the UK Anti-Doping Agency.

c) Testing

All competitors should be aware that random samples may be taken for testing from both themselves and/or their horse/pony. The protocol used will be that of the relevant adult discipline.

Competitors and their horses/ponies at national or international level may be subject to blood tests in line with the Sports Council Policy on illegal and prescribed substances. All young people competing at these levels should be made aware of this

Reporting

i) Anyone who has reasonable grounds for suspecting that a Member is using or selling an illegal substance must report their concerns to the District Commissioner/Centre Proprietor as soon as practicable. If there is an immediate risk to the health, safety or welfare of one or more Members then the Police must be informed as soon as possible. The person reporting their concerns must ensure that any material evidence is retained and should not influence any police investigation.

ii) Upon receiving a report of suspected use or selling of an illegal substance, the District Commissioner/Centre Proprietor should carry out an immediate investigation of the incident and the circumstances in which it occurred, and then decide upon the appropriate action to be taken. This will include:

- Informing the Member's parents/guardians
- Informing The Pony Club Area Representative who in turn will inform The Pony Club Office
- Informing the Police
- Suspending the Member concerned while investigations are completed
- Awaiting the completion of Police investigations and actions

9.   DISQUALIFICATION

Rough or dangerous riding, deliberate interference, unseemly behaviour, or unauthorised changes of tack, etc., may be penalised by disqualification of the rider or team from the next race, the event concerned or the whole competition, at the discretion of the Official Steward, and reported to the Mounted Games Committee, District Commissioner / Centre Proprietor, Area Representative and the Training Chairman. Any reported riders will be recorded and monitored.

10.   SPONSORSHIP

In the case of horses, riders and owners, no form of advertising – and this includes a sponsor's name - may appear on the competitor's or horse's clothing and equipment at any Pony Club competition. This does not preclude the wearing of clothing for horses and riders that has been presented by sponsors of The Pony Club Championships in the current or previous years.

11.   INSURANCE

The Pony Club 'Public and Products Liability Insurance' Policy includes cover for all the official Area Competitions and the Championships. Details of this insurance are available on The Pony Club website.

In the event of any accident, loss or damage occurring to a third party or to the property of a third party (including the general public and competitors) no liability should be admitted, and full details should be sent at once to The Pony Club Office.

The following statements should be included in all event schedules:

12.   HEALTH & SAFETY

Organisers of this event have taken reasonable precautions to ensure the health and safety of everyone present. For these measures to be effective, everyone must take all reasonable precautions to avoid and prevent accidents occurring and must obey the instructions of the organisers and all the officials and stewards.

13.   LEGAL LIABILITY

Save for the death or personal injury caused by the negligence of the organisers, or anyone for whom they are in law responsible, neither the organisers of this event or The Pony Club nor any agent, employee or representative of these bodies, nor the landlord or their tenant, accepts any liability for any accident, loss, damage, injury or illness to horses, owners, riders, spectators, land, cars, their contents and accessories, or any other person or property whatsoever. Entries are only accepted on this basis.

PART 2 - RULES FOR MOUNTED GAMES COMPETITIONS

The competitions will be run in stages. The first will be the Area Competitions to be completed by 27th May 2024. The second will be the Zone Finals, and the third/fourth stages will be at The Pony Club Championships and the Horse of the Year Show (HOYS). Format of all competitions will be run as Seniors followed by Juniors and then the Pairs. Novice Juniors can be run at Area level subject to teams being available and will be run sometime during the day as arranged by the organising branch.

14.   PRINCE PHILIP CUP (SENIOR) TEAMS

The full Branch/Centre team consists of:

a)   Four or Five riders who must be active Members of the stated Branch/Centre of The Pony Club. All team members must have been Members of The Pony Club at the closing date for entries to the competition and at the date of the relevant competition to be eligible to compete at Area qualifying competitions, Zone Finals and The Pony Club Championships.

Members must not have attained their 15th birthday prior to the beginning of the current calendar year (i.e. they must have been born in the year 2009 or later).

Note: Some games require a fifth member (on foot) to hold equipment. At HOYS some games require 5 riders and 5 ponies.

b)   A sixth Member may be nominated, they may only be used to hold equipment in races where all five take part, and then only in the case of injury to one of the other team members. The sixth Member must be eligible under the Rules of the competition, named on the declaration form and attend the turnout inspection correctly dressed for the competition. The declared 6th Member for a Senior Team may be a Junior even if there are already 2 Juniors forming part of that Senior Team. A sixth Member is non-riding and would only be used to hold equipment.

c)   Four or five ponies, at least 4 years old and not exceeding 148cm. A horse or pony shall be deemed to reach the age of 1 on the 1st January following the date on which it is foaled and shall be deemed to become a year older on each successive 1st January.

d)   Dressed to compete

▸   A rider weighing over 54kg may not ride a pony 128cm or under.

- A rider weighing over 60kg may not ride a pony 133cm or under.
- A rider weighing over 66kg may not ride a pony 138cm or under.

If any team Member changes to a different pony during the competition, the same height/weight rules apply.

Note: There is no upper rider weight limit, however, the Mounted Games Committee will monitor riders and ponies and will have the discretion to disqualify any rider considered to be unsuitably mounted.

e) Pony Measurement is without shoes (1¼ cm is deducted when the pony is shod) Official Joint Measurement Board Ltd height Certificates will be accepted (in accordance with current JMB rules) but if there is an objection the Official Steward may measure the pony and their decision is final.

f) Normally four riders and ponies take part in each event, so the riders and/or ponies may be changed for the different events. The fifth rider and/ or pony may be substituted for the final in any race.

g) Members of the teams and ponies may be changed between the Area Meeting, Zone Finals, The Pony Club Championships and HOYS.

h) No pony or rider can compete for more than one Branch/Centre in any one competition year.

i) An adult or senior Member of the Branch/Centre aged 18 or over will be appointed as Team Trainer, whose duties are to take charge of the team outside the arena and to send the team in immediately when called. The Team Trainer may not enter the arena to help or to coach the team.

15.   COMBINED TEAMS

Members from a Branch/Centre unable to raise a complete team may combine with another Branch/Centre from within their Area to form a combined team. A combined team may consist of riders and ponies who would be eligible under these rules to compete in a Branch/ Centre team or of riders who would be ineligible only because the rider was not a Member of the Pony Club as required by rule 14(a)

A combined team which consists entirely of riders who, and ponies which, would otherwise be eligible to compete in a Branch/ Centre team, will be eligible to score points and qualify for finals and overall placings. A combined team which contains one or more riders or ponies which would not be eligible to compete other by virtue of this rule may not qualify for finals or overall placings. A combined team cannot qualify for the Zone Final (see note at end of this rule), but their inclusion in the Area Competition will contribute to the overall number of qualifying teams from Area to Zone. A combined team may only be created with the permission of all District Commissioners/Centre Proprietors concerned and the Area Representative. Teams must have practised together at least once before the Area competition and the Area Competition Entry Form must be fully completed naming the Team Trainer and District Commissioner/Centre Proprietor/ Representative with overall responsibility for the combined team.

NB. In exceptional circumstances if an eligible combined team can demonstrate that both Branches/Centres cannot make up a team, and this is confirmed by the Mounted Games Committee and by both DC/ CP signing the appropriate Declaration Form, they will be allowed to go forward to Zone Finals, however combined teams would be unable to progress further to The Pony Club Championships or qualify for HOYS. Combined Teams would be reviewed every year and Branches/Centres will be encouraged to seek new Members to compete as a Branch/Centre Team.

16.   TRANSFER OF MEMBERS

a) Members wishing to transfer between Branches/Centres to compete in Mounted Games are actively discouraged from doing as it is believed that this is not in the interests of The Pony Club as a whole and the sport of Mounted Games in particular.

b) Any member who transfers from one Branch/Centre to another as a result of a Transfer Request submitted subsequent to the meeting of the Mounted Games Committee held on 10th August 2023 will be ineligible to represent their new Branch/Centre in the Area Competition of the Prince Philip Cup or any of the subsequent qualifying stages for the Prince Philip Cup for a period of 14 months.

c) Any member who transfers from one Branch/Centre to another as a result of a Transfer Request submitted subsequent to the meeting of the Mounted Games Committee held 4th October 2023 will be ineligible to represent their new Branch/Centre in the Area Competition of the Junior Competition or any of the subsequent qualifying stages for Junior Competition for a period of 14 months.

d) Any member ineligible under rule 16.b or 16.c to represent their Branch/Centre at an Area Competition shall not be eligible to compete at the later stages of the Competition during that year.

NB. For the avoidance of doubt, no part of this rule applies to the Pairs competition.

17.   AREA COMPETITIONS

Area Competitions will be arranged to take place by **27th May 2024** at venues selected by Area Representatives and will be organised solely by the Branch/ Centre organising the competition, including the taking of entry forms and entry fees. All Branch/Centre teams will compete at their own Area Competition. Under normal circumstances no more than six teams may compete in any heat or final, but if entries so dictate seven teams may run. The Organiser must consult the Official Steward BEFORE this is implemented and receive his/her permission.

Where there are 18 teams or fewer, each game will consist of 3 heats and a final of 6 teams. Where there are 12 teams or fewer, each game will consist of 2 heats and a final of 6 teams.

Semi-finals must not be run unless there are more than 18 teams entered.

In Areas where more than 18 teams are entered, at the discretion of the Organiser and the Official Steward, the Competition may be divided into two separate sections, normally in the morning and afternoon. The Area Organiser will notify the teams when they are to compete.

It is recommended that the Turnout Inspection for teams competing in the afternoon section can be held during the end of the morning competition.

At each Area Competition the teams will compete against each other in eight events, as listed in this Rule Book.

a)   Declarations: Forms are available as a download from the Mounted Games page on the website. On the day of the competition, the Declaration form giving the names and PELHAM Membership numbers of the members in the team, their ponies details including passport number and PELHAM Coach Accreditation number of the Team Trainer with a certificate of their eligibility signed by the DC must be given to the Organiser of the Competition and to The Pony Club Official Steward. Teams who do not produce a valid and correct Declaration Form or should a breach of eligibility subsequently be discovered the team may be disqualified. Teams being invited to Zones and Championships will be done via contact details on the Declaration Form, please ensure they are clearly printed. Only declared members and ponies are eligible to compete on the day.

b)   Scoring: Every Team completing a Heat will score one point. In the Final, the winning team will score the same number of points as the number of teams competing.

Teams eliminated in a Heat will score NO points.

Teams eliminated in a Final will score NO points (but will retain the point from their heat).

Note: In the case of elimination for any reason, the teams will be placed last of those competing and will score NO points.

c) **Ties:** In the case of equality for qualifying places from a heat to a final only the teams concerned will re-run the race.

In the case of a tie in a final the points will be divided between the teams concerned. In the case of equality for final overall placings at an event the teams concerned will run-off in the tie-break race.

d) **Qualifiers:**

    i. In Area Competitions where 18 or more teams compete on the day, six teams qualify for the Zone Finals.

    ii. In Areas where 15-17 teams compete, five teams will qualify.

    iii. In Areas where 11-14 teams compete, four teams will qualify.

    iv. In Areas where 8-10 teams compete, three teams will qualify.

    v. In Areas where fewer than 8 teams compete, two teams will qualify. A number of teams may be selected, depending on the number of teams competing at Area Competitions to make up the number competing at each Zone Final to between 14 and 21 teams.

Those required will be allocated to a Zone Final. When a Zone Competition is over-subscribed Branches/Centres will be allocated to the nearest available Zone Competition at the discretion of the Mounted Games Committee.

Should a team withdraw from a Zone Final; the place will be offered to the next highest placed team, depending on the number of teams competing at Area Competitions.

e) **Zone Finals:** FOUR Zone Finals will be arranged to take place in June/July.

At Zone Finals teams will compete against each other in 10 Events and Finals as listed in this Rule Book.

The winning team from each Zone Final will qualify for HOYS.

f) **Runners-up Competition:** Branches/Centres placed 2nd to 7th at Zone Finals will compete for the final two HOYS places at The Pony Club Championships. Scoring heats may be used in the initial phase of the competition.

Any rider or pony that competed in a Branch/Centre Team which qualified for HOYS at Zone Finals in the current year may not compete again in the Senior Runners-Up competitions at The JCB Pony Club Championships at Offchurch Bury, Offchurch, Leamington Spa, Warwickshire, CV33 9AW.

►   Runners-up Competition – Sunday 11th August 2024

g)   **Intermediate Championship:** The next THREE placed teams at each Zone Final not qualifying for the Championships after all the allocations have been made, will be invited to the Intermediate Championships at The Pony Club Championships in August.

Any rider or pony that competed in a Branch/Centre Team which qualified for HOYS or that competes in The Pony Club Mounted Games Senior Runners-up competitions in the current year, cannot also compete at Intermediate Championships at The JCB Pony Club Championships at Offchurch Bury, Offchurch, Leamington Spa, Warwickshire, CV33 9AW.

►   Intermediate Championship – Saturday 10th August 2024

18.   JUNIOR COMPETITION

a)   **Format:** A three-round competition consisting of Area qualifiers and Junior Zone Finals to be held in conjunction with the present Prince Philip Cup Senior Competitions at these levels and a National Final at The Pony Club Championships.

b)   **Teams:** As PPC Competition Rules, except:

i.   Riders must not have attained their 11th birthday prior to the beginning of the current calendar year (i.e. born in the year of 2013 or after).

ii.   Members/ponies eligible for a Junior Team can make up the numbers in a Prince Philip Cup Senior team up to a maximum of two Members and/or two ponies. For example, two Members and/or ponies from a Junior Team can compete in a Senior A Team, additionally two Members and/or ponies from the same Junior Team can compete in a Senior B Team. This does not apply to a Junior Member who is used as the non-riding 6th Member in a Prince Philip Cup Team.

The Entry Form, which must be signed by the District Commissioner, should be sent together with the entry fee to the Secretary of the organising Branch/Centre. Entry fees should be set at a reasonable level by the Area in order to cover competition costs. A Start Fee may be charged if necessary.

The Line Stewards nominated for the PPC Competition will also be required to officiate at the Junior and Pairs Competitions.

c) **Declarations:** Forms are available as a download from the Mounted Games page on the website. On the day of the competition, the Declaration form giving the names and PELHAM Membership numbers of the members in the team, their ponies details including passport number and PELHAM Coach Accreditation number of the Team Trainer with a certificate of their eligibility signed by the DC must be given to the Organiser of the Competition and to The Pony Club Official Steward. Teams who do not produce a valid and correct Declaration Form or should a breach of eligibility subsequently be discovered the team may be disqualified. Teams being invited to Zones and Championships will be done via contact details on the Declaration Form, please ensure they are clearly printed. Only declared members and ponies are eligible to compete on the day.

d) **Area Competitions:** As for PPC Competition Rules.

i. Should an Area wish to hold its Area Junior Competition separately from its Area PPC event this is permitted with the agreement of the Area Representative and the Official Steward.
ii. The number of qualifiers from each Area Competition to their respective Zone Final will be as for the Prince Philip Cup Competition.
iii. At all events the Prince Philip Cup Competition will be run first.

e) **Junior Zone Finals:** Four Zone Finals will take place in conjunction with the PPC Zone Finals. Each Junior Zone Final will usually consist of 14 to 21 teams.

The allocation of Areas to each Zone Final will be determined by the Mounted Games Committee on a similar basis as the PPC Competition and will remain as such, subject to any alterations deemed necessary each year within these criteria.

Branches/Centres with teams that qualify for the Zone Finals will be notified in June of the date and place of the Zone Final at which they are to compete. Full details will be sent to them as soon as possible.

f) **National Final – The JCB Pony Club Championships - Offchurch Bury, Offchurch, Leamington Spa, Warwickshire, CV33 9AW**

The top 7 Teams from each of the Zones will compete in the National Junior

Final. Full details of this competition will be handed to the qualifying Teams at their Zone Final.

- Junior Championships – Friday 9th August 2024

19. PAIRS COMPETITION

- Members must have attained their 11th birthday prior to the beginning of the current calendar year and must not have attained their 19th birthday by the beginning of the current calendar year.
- Members must be from the same Pony Club Area, can be from the same Branch, or a mix of two branches, or Centres.
- Mixed pairs will be called by the Branch name or both Branches or Branch/Centre names.
- Members may compete in both the Pairs and PPC Competitions.
- Members and Ponies may be substituted.
- Height/Weight rules as per the PPC and Junior competitions.
- NB There is no upper rider weight limit, however, the Mounted Games Committee will monitor riders and ponies and will have the discretion to disqualify any rider considered to be unsuitably mounted.
- All General Rules will apply where applicable.
- All heats will be scored with no finals.
- **Coloured hat bands may be used for Pairs competition**
- Final results will be decided by overall total of points scored from heats.
- Drawn Order, where more than 7 pairs are entered, heats will be run and scored with the winning pair scoring the same number of points as the number of pairs competing in the largest heat.

Qualifiers (Area Competitions):

- Where 18 or more pairs compete on the day 6 pairs will qualify
- Where 15-17 pairs compete on the day 5 pairs will qualify
- Where 11-14 pairs compete on the day 4 pairs will qualify
- Where 8-10 pairs compete on the day 3 pairs will qualify
- Where fewer than 8 pairs compete, 2 pairs will qualify
- Depending on the number of pairs teams competing at Area Competitions additional qualifying places may be allocated to make up the number competing at Zone Finals at the discretion of the Mounted Games Committee.

Notes for Pairs Competitions:

- Pairs Qualify from Area to Zone to Championships
- Pairs final will be on the same day as the Intermediate Competition at the Championships

Pairs Final – The JCB Pony Club Championships - Offchurch Bury, Offchurch, Leamington Spa, Warwickshire CV33 9AW

▸ The top 6 Pairs from each of the Zones will compete in the Pairs Final. Full details of this competition will be handed to the qualifying Pairs at their Zone Final.

▸ Pairs Final – Saturday 10th August 2024

Games: The games rules will follow the Area/Zone/Championship rules adapted to suit pairs.

Declarations: Pairs forms are available as a download from the Mounted Games page on the website. On the day of the competition, the Declaration form giving the names and PELHAM Membership numbers of the members in the pair, their ponies details including passport number and PELHAM Coach Accreditation number of the Team Trainer with a certificate of their eligibility signed by the DC must be given to the Organiser of the Competition and to The Pony Club Official Steward. Pairs who do not produce a valid and correct Declaration Form or should a breach of eligibility subsequently be discovered the pair may be disqualified. Pairs being invited to Zones and Championships will be done via contact details on the Declaration Form, please ensure they are clearly printed. Only declared members and ponies are eligible to compete on the day.

20. GUIDELINES FOR JUNIOR/NOVICE COMPETITION - AREA COORDINATORS

Main areas of focus for Area Coordinators (page 4):

1) To give support to the Official Steward at the Area Mounted Games competition.

2) To respond to any branch or centre request for help in starting up Mounted Games or a branch or centre request to give some initial help with grass roots and novice teams, riders and their team trainer.

3) Work with the Area Representative and Branches and Centres in the Area to enable them to offer Mounted Games. This should be done by being a source of advice and support to help understanding of the game and by helping them find coaches and equipment.

4) Support the development of Mounted Games within the Area. To help promote branches and centres to start up grass roots & novice 'Give it a Go' taster Rallies and fun training days.

5) Where possible, to help branches to organise Area training events

which are open to all Pony Club members from within the Area.

6)   Act as a point of contact within the Area for Parents, Guardians, members and Branches/ Centres who want to know about the sport of Mounted Games and opportunities to play it.

b) JUNIOR/NOVICE COMPETITION - These competitions are envisaged as a preliminary step for children wishing to compete at Area Pony Club Mounted Games. The spirit of the novice games is about encouraging children to take part and achieve, with suitable support and simplified races. **Area Coordinators are there to provide help and support.**

This may be organised as a lead rein competition and children that are managing novice games competently will progress quickly into Junior/ PPC mounted games teams. The aim is safe, encouraging fun!

Novice level competitions can be run very successfully as part of Branch/ Centre friendly competitions using the same arena and equipment. To help children start to learn mounted games rules, competitions should be run according to The Pony Club Mounted Games Rule Book, with some additional guidelines:

Note: This competition is for Members learning the skills and rules of Pony Club Games (who may need a leader). A list of suggested games can be found on the Mounted Games page of the website, these games are proposed so to help provide different skills to help develop riders and ponies for future Mounted Games competitions.

1.   Ponies may be ridden in any normal riding bit with a single rein, excluding English gags and bitless bridles (grass reins may be used)

2.   Trainers are allowed to be with their team and talk the Members through the races.

3.   Ponies may be led, but help may only be given by the leader for safety reasons.

4.   A leader may leg up children too small to mount.

5.   Children should correct their errors, dismounting if necessary, but may be helped to remount.

6.   The safety of the children and ponies is paramount and it is the responsibility of the trainers and DC's to ensure that children are suitably mounted.

7.   It is recommended that heats are scored according to placings rather

than heats and finals.

8. Members who are confidently competing at novice level should be
    encouraged to compete at Area Competitions (Junior/PP Cup)

9. Entry Fees to be kept by the organising Branch.

21.   FRIENDLY BRANCH COMPETITIONS AND EXTERNAL EVENTS

a) Branch Friendly Competitions

Friendly Mounted Games competitions can be organised by Branches
and Centres for all ages and abilities. They may be for teams, pairs and
individuals (including lead reins).

**These friendly competitions are usually open to any Pony Club team,
pairs and individuals wishing to apply to the organizing Branch/Centre.**

**Combined teams are allowed subject to agreement of the organizing
Branch/Centre.**

**All Branch Friendly Mounted Games competitions must be publicised
on the Pony Club Website.**

The Mounted Games Rule Book should provide a framework for the
organisation of these competitions, however, the format and choice of
games should reflect the age, competence, size and experience of members
and ponies.

All Friendly Games Competitions organised in accordance with this Rule
Book should be organised by a Branch with the knowledge and permission
of the District Commissioner and Branch Committee.

Notice should also be given to the Area Representative and/or the local
Member of the Mounted Games Committee **or Mounted Games Area
Coordinator.**

The directions outlined above as to the running of Area Competitions may
be taken as best practice for the organisation of a Games Friendly although,
of course, there will be no Headquarters involvement; accordingly, the
appointment of an Official Steward and of Line Stewards, the supply of
rosettes, and the financing, will be matters solely for the organising Branch.

The importance of the appointment of experienced officials cannot be
overemphasised. Quite apart from the directions on safety for the Area
Competitions given above, the general rules and principles as to health,

safety and risk assessment, which apply to all Branches/Centres in the organisation of events, will be applicable to Friendly Competitions.

The Risk Assessment carried out by the organising Branch will be particularly relevant to the appropriate level of First Aid cover.

b) External Events: County Shows, Trade Shows, or other Major Equestrian Events

It is accepted that Pony Club Mounted Games Team Competitions are sometimes run outside the Branch/Centre network, typically at shows or other major equestrian events. **These events may be by invitation only.**

- **Planned Pony Club** attendance at external events must be notified to The Pony Club Office/Area Representative, a**nd their permission may be required.**
- **All County Shows, Trade Shows, or other major equine events must be publicised on the Pony Club Website.**
- **Combined or mixed teams may be invited to participate to make up numbers if required by the event.**
- A Pony Club Official must be appointed to take overall charge and responsibility.
- The Pony Club Official must carry out proper risk assessments in accordance with Pony Club guidelines.
- The Pony Club Official should ask to see a copy of the event's own Risk Assessment.
- The Pony Club Official must ensure that risk assessments cover all aspects eg arena, collecting ring, horse walks, overnight stays, penning, practice areas etc.
- The Pony Club Official must record and report any accidents/ incidents to The Pony Club Office.

Any Health and Safety concerns Organisers have prior to, during or after the event should be raised directly with the office.

c) Home Internationals: RWHS and other invited competitions.

Held annually at Royal Windsor Horse Show, the DAKS Home International Mounted Games Championships is an invitational competition which sees Pony Club members from England, Scotland, Wales, Northern Ireland, and Republic of Ireland. Dates for National Selection Trials can be found on the website and at the rear of this rulebook under 'Fixtures'.

DCs and Centre Proprietors are invited to nominate members for National Selection Trials to compete at RWHS and any other invited

competition.

- ▸ Members must have obtained their C test before the date of their nomination.
- ▸ The Pony ridden at the Trial must be the one the member will ride at RWHS and any other International competition.
- ▸ The nominee should be a good games player, team member and representative of their Branch/Centre and Country.
- ▸ Members must be free from any restriction imposed under the Transfer Rule by the closing date of the nominations.
- ▸ Only those members who will be eligible to compete in their Area competition can attend a Selection Trial.
- ▸ Nominations for Selection Trials may differ between countries, check selection criteria on nomination form.

d) INTERNATIONAL MOUNTED GAMES EXCHANGE (IMGE)

The Mounted Games International Exchange provides Pony Club members from across the world to visit other countries with their sport and take part in Competition, Cultural experiences, and social activities.

DCs and Centre Proprietors are invited to nominate one member for the International Mounted Games Exchange between Great Britain, Australia, Canada & USA.

- ▸ Members must have obtained their C+ test before the date of their nomination.
- ▸ Members must have their 16th birthday within the year of the exchange.
- ▸ The nominee should be a good games player, team member and representative of their Branch/Centre and Country.
- ▸ Members must be free from any restriction imposed under the Transfer Rule by the closing date of the nominations.
- ▸ DCs and Centre Proprietors will provide a confidential character reference.
- ▸ DCs and Centre Proprietors will be asked to include a copy of the Branch/Centre Programmes and clearly mark those rallies & events the member has attended and/or include a report from PELHAM of their member's record of achievements and attendance in the past two years.

22.   GENERAL RULES

The following rules will apply in all events unless stated to the contrary in the rules for a particular event.

a) **Entries:** Each Branch/Centre of The Pony Club in Great Britain may enter any number of teams for all Area Competitions.

The Entry Form, which **MUST** be signed by the District Commissioner, should be sent together with the entry fee to the Secretary of the organising Branch/Centre.

Entry fees should be set at a reasonable level by the organising Branch/Centre in order to cover competition costs. A Start Fee may be charged if necessary to help with First Aid cover.

Each Branch/Centre will also nominate two experienced Line Stewards per Team who will officiate at the Area Competitions. A form for these nominations will be sent by the Organiser to Team Trainers together with Area Competition details. On completion, the form must be returned to the Organiser. See also Instructions for Line Stewards – APPENDIX F.

Branches/Centres withdrawing from Area Competitions after entering must inform the Organiser not fewer than 48 hours prior to the competition. If later than this their entry fee may be retained by the organising Branch/Centre.

If a Branch/Centre makes an entry and then wishes to withdraw, 50% of the entry fee will be refunded by the organising Branch/ Centre provided notice is received by the Organiser 10 or more days before the competition.

b) **Withdrawals (All competitions & Championships)**

If a Branch or Centre withdraws a team or individual prior to the closing date for a competition, a full refund of entry and stabling fees will be made, less an administration charge. Withdrawals after the closing date for a competition will not be refunded.

c) **Abandonment (All competitions & Championships)**

In the event of a competition being abandoned, for whatever reason, a refund of 50% of the entry fee will be given. In such an instance the refund process will be communicated and must be followed.

d) **Substitutions:** Any pony/rider injured before the start of a race may be substituted by the nominated 5th pony/rider, even if the injury occurs whilst on the start line.

e) **Declarations:** Forms are available as a download from the Mounted Games page on the website. On the day of the competition, the Declaration form giving the names and PELHAM Membership numbers of the members in the team, their ponies details including passport number and PELHAM Coach Accreditation number of the Team Trainer with a certificate of their eligibility signed by the DC must be given to the Organiser of the Competition and to The Pony Club Official Steward. Teams who do not produce a valid and correct Declaration Form or should a breach of eligibility subsequently be discovered the team may be disqualified. Teams being invited to Zones and Championships will be done via contact details on the Declaration Form, please ensure they are clearly printed. Only declared members and ponies are eligible to compete on the day.

f) **Inspection:** It is the competitors' responsibility to ensure that their tack is in accordance with the rules and that they present themselves for inspection. Riders and ponies will be inspected before the start in the clothing and saddlery in which they are to compete and these will not be changed thereafter without reference to the Official Steward, failure to do so may entail disqualification from the Competition. Turnout Judges will report any Riders whom they think may be over-weight for their ponies.

Any unusual decoration of the horse with unnatural things, such as ribbons, flowers, glitter etc. in the mane/tail or applied to the coat is forbidden. Red bows should be worn in the tail of ponies that kick.

g) **Initial Parade:** In all rounds, teams will parade in the arena at the commencement of the competition, when rosettes will be presented to the first three teams in the Turnout Competition.

h) **Objections:** Only District Commissioners or Centre Proprietors or their appointed representatives **named on the Declaration Form** are entitled to make requests for information or to lodge objections, which must be made promptly verbally to the Official Steward.

If a District Commissioner/Centre Proprietor is unable to be present, they must appoint an experienced person, preferably a senior member of the Branch/Centre Committee, to deputise for them and this person must be nominated on the Declaration Form. This may not be the team trainer/ team manager or the parent of a competitor.

No objection will be allowed to the starting, judging or stewarding of any event. Any other objection arising out of a heat or final must be made and if possible, decided upon before the start of the next heat or final.

An objection to the equipment or layout of the Arena must be made not later than half an hour before the start of the Competition.

An objection to the weight of a rider may be made at any time during the Competition.

To prevent disruption during the competition, an objection to the qualification of a rider or a pony must be made as soon as possible before the commencement of the Competition. Should a breach of eligibility subsequently be discovered, then the Mounted Games Committee may disqualify the offending team, even if after the Competition.

An objection arising out of the final result must be lodged before the awards are made.

Video evidence will not be considered. If the Official Steward cannot give a decision on the day, they may refer the matter to the Mounted Games Committee for adjudication.

23.   JUDGES AND OFFICIALS

a)   **Judges of Turnout:** Judges can be selected from the senior Officials or they can be specially appointed by the Organiser. It is recommended that the Area Representatives and someone familiar with Mounted Games Turnout are invited to judge. The Turnout Judges will attend the Initial Parade to ensure no item of tack/clothing has been changed since their inspection.

Rosettes will be awarded to the three Best Turned Out Teams on the basis of serviceability, safety, cleanliness, and neatness of pony, rider and tack rather than uniformity. A timetable notifying Branches/ Centres when their team will be inspected is recommended, particularly in inclement weather. See Turnout Competition.

Team trainers or their nominee must accompany their teams during the inspection.

Organisers will provide a steward for the Judges inspecting Turnout, who will make a note of any faults.

b)   **Official Steward:** An Official Steward will be appointed by The Mounted Games Committee for Area Competitions, Zone Finals and Finals. They supervise the Briefing. Their duties are to adjudicate on objections, to decide on eliminations and generally to ensure that the competition is run in accordance with the Rules. They may replace a Line Steward if considered necessary.

They may, on their own initiative, "object" and take action on any matter which comes to their notice. Their decision is final and binding.

c)   **Line Judges:** The Judges decide the order in which the competitors cross the finishing line. The Judges are not responsible for infringements. At Zone Finals, however, the Judges will liaise with the Official Steward on Start/ Finish Line infringements. The Judges receive reports of eliminations from the Official Steward and taking these into consideration give the results of each heat and final. The Judges should position themselves at the same end of the finishing line as the Commentator for easy liaison.

d)   Line Stewards: There must be two Line Stewards for each lane at Area Competitions. The positioning and duties of Line Stewards are set out in APPENDIX F. For each lane the Steward is to be standing at the top of the Arena in line with each line. If there are not enough Line Stewards available on the day, the Official Steward can adopt the following rule as used at Zone finals. At Zone Finals and Championships Line Stewards are appointed by the committee and will be neutral, there may only be two or four Line Stewards positioned at the Start/Finish Line, therefore any errors will not be boarded at this end.

The Line Steward Co-ordinator (if appointed) organises and supervises the rotation of stewards before and during the competition and reports any problems to the Official Steward. For the Pairs Competition ONLY, there may be TWO experienced Line Stewards on the Start Line and TWO at the changeover end.

e)   Starter: The instructions of the Starter are set out in APPENDIX E.

f)   Judges' Writers (Two are advised, one for each Judge): The Judge's Writer fills in the results of each heat and final on the Judge's Slips (obtainable by the Organiser from The Pony Club Shop) and takes these promptly to the Announcer and Scorer. These slips must be retained by the Organiser.

g)   Scorer: The Scorer keeps the scores on the Official Sheet. A scoreboard may be displayed. The Official score sheets must be sent to The Pony Club Office by the Official Steward at the end of the competition.

h)   Announcer: The Announcer should give a short explanation of each event. They call in the teams for each heat and final and they announce colours and positions at the start. They announce the results of heats and finals and gives aggregate scores of the teams after each event.

i)   Collecting Ring Stewards: They keep order in the Collecting Ring and get teams ready to send them into the Arena when required. They should deal through the Team Trainers, who must remain in the Collecting Ring. Any difficulty in the Collecting Ring should be reported immediately to the Official Steward.

Note: Only the Team Trainer and ONE other person aged 18 years old or over may be in the collecting ring with their team, and should stand in the 'trainers track' if one is available.

j) **Arena Party:** The Arena Party puts up and issues equipment and ensures that everything is ready for each event, removing the equipment when it is no longer required – SEE APPENDIX E

k) **Equipment Steward:** There should be one Equipment Steward to ensure all equipment is ready before the competition starts and check that all equipment is placed correctly for each race.

24. THE COMPETITION

a) **The Start:** The signal to start will be the drop of a flag. The starter may order an unruly pony to stand behind the 6m line.

The starter alone is responsible that the start is fair, so if, after dropping their flag, they consider the start was unfair, they must immediately raise the flag again and recall the riders, by whistle.

b) **Mounted Definitions: Riders must remain mounted at all times when in the arena unless taking part in a race which necessitates them dismounting and must leave the arena mounted. Failure to comply with this rule will incur elimination.** Except when the rules allow riders to dismount, they must remain mounted (facing forward, legs astride the saddle, or back when saddles are not used). Reins must be always over (not under) the pony's head. Should one fall off and lose their pony, they must remount unaided and resume the race as near as possible to the place where they fell off.

JUNIOR COMPETITION ONLY: Riders in difficulty must have made a reasonable attempt to re-mount before seeking help from a Line Steward or a fellow Team Member.

  i.   Riders may lead their pony to the changeover end where the Line Steward may hold the pony whilst they remount.
  ii. Riders may lead their pony to the start/finish line where a fellow mounted team member may hold the pony whilst they re-mount. In a Heat – Any Team receiving help to remount will score ONE Point, but WILL NOT qualify for the Final.
  iii. Any additional help from a steward e.g. picking up equipment, leg-up etc. will entail elimination.
  iv. In a Final – Any Team receiving help to remount will score ONE Point only.

**c)	Loose Ponies:** Loose ponies leaving the arena entail elimination. If a rider deliberately let's go of the pony, e.g. to replace equipment, the team may be eliminated from the event at the discretion of the Official Steward. No person may enter the ring to catch a loose pony. Providing it is safe to do so, **any person in the arena may catch a loose pony only when the pony has left the playing area. They may hand it back to the rider or another member of the team but may not help in any other way**. The team may then continue from where the infringement took place.

**d)	The result:** The result of a race will be decided by the order in which the ponies' heads cross the finishing line when ridden or the riders cross the line when dismounted (as in the Sack Race). When ponies finish in pairs, it is the head of the second pony which counts.

**e)	After a race:** Riders will stay in the arena when they have finished their parts in an event and must not ride down the course until all teams have completed the event and are signalled to do so by the starter. Competitors must leave the Arena at walk.

**f)	Pony Encouragement:** The hand, the reins or other article may not be used as a whip.

**g)	6m Box:**

  i.	At a changeover, the next rider to start must take up position in the 6m box. They must go next and may not be replaced by one of the others for any reason. The remainder of the team must be behind the 6m line.
  ii.	Handovers from one rider to the next must take place behind the line (i.e. the whole of the outgoing rider and his pony must be behind the line until the incoming rider and their pony have crossed it). Should the outgoing rider cross the line too soon, their team will be eliminated unless they return to correct the error.

**h)	Backing Off:**

Deliberate backing off behind the 6m line or indeed any other action by the next rider at a Changeover which facilitates a "flying" changeover is not permitted. The Official Steward may eliminate a team which seeks to take this advantage.

**i)	Change Overs:**

  i.	No rider may help another unless they are both involved in a Change Over.
  ii.	When correcting mistakes, only the rider/s concerned should be

in the field of play. All other riders must remain behind the line. However, should a rider/pony step accidentally into the field of play during a race, the team will not be penalised providing the error is corrected promptly.

iii. A Team Member may assist another by leading a pony UP TO the 6m line, but may NOT lead them INTO the 6m box.

iv. At the Change Over, should the article be dropped, only the incoming rider may pick it up and hand it to the outgoing rider. They may dismount to do this or remain mounted.

j)   Retrieving articles dropped or upset

i. No article may be put in the mouth, on penalty of elimination.

ii. Should a rider drop an article they have to carry, they may dismount or remain mounted to pick it up by hand, after which they must remount to resume the event from where the article was dropped.

iii. When a rider has made a reasonable attempt to put an article they are carrying into or to remove an article from a container or to place an article on or to take it off a table, pole etc and drops the article in the process, they must pick it up mounted or dismounted and if appropriate place it where it needs to go. This may be done mounted or dismounted. If dismounted they should then re-mount and continue the race.

iv. When correcting an error, dismounted, the rider must continue to hold the pony by the rein throughout.

v. If any equipment becomes dislodged after the incoming rider has crossed the line, then the outgoing rider must correct it and then return to start their part in the race.

k)   Correcting Errors: Should a rider knock over a container, table, post etc. while making a reasonable attempt to put an article they are carrying where it needs to go, the rider must replace the knocked over equipment where it should go.

This may be done mounted or dismounted. The rider should then put in place the article they are carrying from either a mounted or dismounted position. If the rider has not made a reasonable attempt to put the article they were carrying in the correct position, then after replacing the knocked over equipment, they must be mounted before placing the article they were carrying in the correct place. The penalty for not correcting properly is elimination from that race.

A rider who commits an error during an event may return to correct it, even after crossing the changeover or finishing line, provided the Official Steward has not declared the race to be over.

l)   Broken Equipment: Any misuse causing broken equipment will entail Elimination. The race will not be re-run.

m)   Bending – Definition: In all races in which the riders weave round bending poles the following will apply:

   a.   The riders may pass the first pole on either the right or the left. Thereafter, they weave alternately to the left and right of successive poles.

   b.   MISSED POLE: Provided a rider returns and rides round the pole they do not need to continue on the same bend as previously.

   c.   The following faults will incur elimination of the team from an event.

      i.   Missing a pole unless corrected.
      ii.   Failure by the rider concerned to replace a pole he had knocked down.

n)   Interference: If any rider or his pony interferes with another Team during an event the offending Team may be eliminated or in serious cases disqualified at the discretion of the Official Steward. Races will not be re-run when a Team upsets the equipment of another Team but the offending Team will be eliminated from the race.

o)   Officials: It is forbidden for anyone other than officials to enter the arena during the competition, except the District Commissioner/Centre Proprietor (or their appointed representative, if they are not able to be present) in order to lodge an objection. Team trainers are not allowed in the arena during the competition.

p)   Race Substitutions: If for any reason an event cannot be run, it may either be replaced by the Spare Event, or be declared void at the discretion of the Official Steward.

25.   EVENTS AREA COMPETITIONS – GAMES

Notes:

1.   Teams should be trained to correct their mistakes and not to play to the Line Stewards' signals. The signals are for the information of the Official Steward.

2.   In the event of an obstruction by any Team, the Line Steward of the

Team causing the obstruction will not signal until the end of the game.

3. The rules for all games concerning the position of equipment, or that of the Number Five holding equipment, are that they must be 3m behind the Changeover line. The position will be marked by a circle.

4. In all cases of broken, dropped or upset equipment, General Rules will apply, unless stated otherwise.

5. In all Events, competitors and their ponies must cross the start, finish and Changeover lines between the corner markers marked with an X on the Arena Plan.

26. PRINCE PHILIP CUP AREA GAMES 2024

EVENT 1: Bending

Five Bending Poles are placed in a line 7 to 9 metres apart. All four riders are mounted at the Start/Finish end.

On the signal to start, Number One, carrying a Baton, rides down and back through the Bending Poles. After crossing the Start/Finish Line, then hands the Baton to Number Two. Numbers Two, Three & Four will similarly ride down and back through the Bending Poles in succession.

The winning team will be the one whose Number Four is first over the Finish Line, mounted, carrying the Baton. Knocked down Poles must be replaced by the rider concerned, they must go back and resume the race from the point where the Pole was knocked down, they can resume by bending either side of the position of the knocked down Pole and not necessarily on the same bend as before.

Line Stewards will not signal unless the bending Pole is broken or lying flat on the ground.

EVENT 2: Equestrian Games 5 Mug – Pole & Mug Specific

A line of five Bending Poles for each team will be put up 7 to 9 metres apart. Pole 1 is the nearest to the Start/Finish Line. A table will be placed 3 metres behind the Changeover Line, one for each team.

All four riders are mounted at the Start/Finish end. Each team will have five mugs, four of these, of which one will have the EGUK Logo on, will be placed INVERTED on the team's table and one will be carried by Number One at the start. The EGUK Mug will be placed at 8 o'clock (left front) looking from the Start/Finish Line on the table.

On the signal to start, Number One rides to pole 2 and places their mug inverted on the top. They then ride to their team's table, pick up another mug (not the EGUK mug) and return to hand it to Number Two behind the Start/Finish Line. Number Two rides to pole 3, Number Three rides to pole 4 and Four rides to pole 5, all riders placing their mug inverted on their pole. Number Four will then place the last mug with the EGUK Logo onto pole Number 1 on their way back to the Finish Line.

The winning team is the one whose Numbers Four is first over the Finish Line with a mug on each pole and the EGUK mug on pole 1.

The riders may ride straight and need not bend through the poles. Any mugs knocked off the table must always be replaced INVERTED by the rider concerned; the EGUK Logo mugs can be replaced inverted anywhere on the table.

EVENT 3: Farmers' Market

A table will be placed level with the first Bending Pole. 3 metres behind the Changeover line each team will have four items (1 string of sausages, 1 potato, 1 egg box, 1 bottle of milk) placed within the circle on the ground. The bottle of milk will be placed upright.

All four riders line up behind the Start/Finish Line. On the signal to start, Number One, carrying a tack box tray, rides and places the tray on the table. They ride to the far end, dismount, pick up any item and remount, return to place the item in the tray and then ride across the Start/Finish Line.

Number Two rides towards the Changeover Line and dismounts, collects any item, remounts, returns to place the item in the tray and crosses the Start/Finish Line.

Number Three repeats the actions of Number Two.

Number Four repeats the actions of Number Two and Three but after placing the final item into the tray, they then pick up and carry the tray containing the 'shopping' over the Finish Line.

The milk bottle must be placed upright in the tray but does not need to remain so once the tray has been collected by Number Four.

The sausages may hang over the edge of the tray. The bottle of milk must remain upright whilst in the circle and when placed into the tray until collected by Number Four.

Items knocked out of the circle other than the bottle should be replaced by the Line Steward concerned.

EVENT 4: PG Sports Pyramid (Spell PGUK)

A table will be placed on the Centre Line, and another placed 3 metres behind the Changeover Line.

On the latter Table will be placed four plastic Cartons weighing 500 grams (un-stacked) each with a printed letter on each side. As you look from the Start/Finish Line they will be placed as follows.

'K' Front right

'U' Back Right

'G' Back Left

'P' Front Left

On the signal to start, Number One rides to the table behind the Changeover Line and collects the Carton with the letter 'K' and places it on the Centre Line table. Number One then returns to cross the Start/ Finish Line.

Number Two rides to the table behind the Changeover Line, collects the Carton with the letter 'U' and stacks this upon the previous Carton placed on the Centre Line table. Number Two then returns to cross the Start/Finish Line.

In turn Numbers Three (Collects 'G') and Four (Collects 'P') and complete in a similar manner and the winning team is the one whose Number Four is first over the Finish Line with all four Cartons stacked on the Centre Line table spelling from the top PGUK.

After collecting a Carton, the rider may adjust the stack by hand or with the Carton before or after placing their Carton on the stack. If the table is knocked over, or a Carton falls, the rider concerned may dismount to replace them in any order on the top table at the Changeover end, the Cartons must be placed side by side but not on top of each other. At the table on the Centre Line the Cartons must be stacked upright and in the correct order.

Line Stewards will only board once the incorrect carton has been placed on the Centre Line table.

EVENT 5: Tyre

A motorcycle Tyre will be placed on the Centre Line for each team.

Numbers One and Two will form up behind the Start/Finish Line, with

Number Four behind the 6 metre Line. Number Three will be behind the Changeover Line.

On the signal to start, Numbers One and Two ride to the Tyre where Number One dismounts, hands their pony to Number Two, gets through the Tyre and remounts. Both riders then continue to the Changeover Line where Number One will wait.

Numbers Two and Three then ride to the Tyre where Number Two dismounts, hands their pony to Number Three, gets through the Tyre and remounts. Both riders then continue to the Start/Finish Line, and Number Two leaves the race.

Number Three joins up with Number Four and they complete the course, with Number Three going through the Tyre, after which they cross the Changeover Line. Number Three drops out and Numbers Four and Number One complete the course, with Number Four going through the Tyre.

The winning team will be the one whose final pair (Numbers One & Four) cross the Finish Line first, mounted on their ponies.

At each changeover, the next pony to go must remain behind the Line until both incoming riders have crossed it.

The rider who is to lead the pony may take hold of the rein behind the Line or as they go down the arena. The pony must be led by the rein nearer the ridden pony and not by the bit ring or any other part of the bridle. The Tyre may not be touched until the pony has been correctly handed over. Riders are not allowed to run with the Tyre.

The Tyre must remain inside of Poles 2 & 3 and in the team's lane throughout the race. If the Tyre rolls or is dragged outside of Poles 2 and 3 in their lane, then the dismounted rider must retrieve it before resuming the race.

EVENT 6: Hollywood Bowl Bottle

There will be two tables for each team, one on the Centre Line and the other 3 metres beyond the Changeover Line. On the latter table there will be a plastic Bottle, weighted with 500 grams of sand.

On the signal to start, Number One, carrying a Bottle, rides to the centre, places it upright on the table, rides to the far end, picks up the Bottle from the table there and returns to hand it to Number Two behind the Start/Finish Line.

Rider Number Two rides to the table at the far end, places the Bottle upright on it, returns to the Centre Line to pick up the Bottle from the table there and hands it to Number Three behind the Start/Finish Line.

Number Three will act in a similar manner to Number One, returning to hand the Bottle from the far end to Number Four.

Number Four will act in a similar manner to Number Two. The winning team will be the one whose Number Four crosses the Finish Line first, mounted and carrying the Bottle. A Bottle knocked over must be replaced UPRIGHT.

EVENT 7: Old Sock

At the changeover end each team will have four socks sewn into balls about the size of a fist, placed on the ground in the circle 3 metres beyond the Changeover Line. Across the Centre will be a row of buckets, one for each team.

All four riders form up behind the Start/Finish line.

On the signal to start, Number One, carrying a sock, rides to their team's bucket and drops the sock into it. They ride towards the Changeover line, dismount, pick up a sock, remount and return to the start to hand it to Number Two.

Numbers Two, Three & Four will complete the course in the same way in succession, with Number Four dropping the last sock into the bucket on their way back.

The winning team will be the one whose Number Four is first over the Finish Line with five socks in the bucket.

Socks knocked out of the circle should be replaced by the Line Steward concerned.

EVENT 8: 5 Flag

A Flag Cone will be placed 3 metres behind the Changeover Line and another on the Centre Line. Each team will have five Flags on Canes. Four of these will be in the team's Flag Cone on the Centre Line and one will be carried by Number One at the start.

On the signal to start Number One rides to the other end of the arena and places the Flag they are carrying into the Flag Cone. They ride back, pick a Flag out of the team's Flag Cone on the Centre Line and hand this Flag to Number Two behind the Start/Finish Line.

Numbers Two, Three and Four will complete the course in the same way up and down the arena in succession so that, at the end, the team will have placed four Flags in the Flag Cone at the far end of the arena and Number Four finishes over the Finish Line mounted and carrying the fifth Flag.

Should the Flag Cone be knocked over, the rider must put it up again, replacing any Flags there may have been in it. Should a rider take more than one Flag from the Flag Cone, they must replace the surplus. They may dismount to correct mistakes.

The winning team is the one whose Number Four is first over the Finish Line carrying the Flag.

If the Flag should come off the Cane, the stick may be used to complete the race.

On windy days rubber bands can be used to keep the Flags furled and prevent them blowing together.

SPARE: 2 Flag

There will be two Flag Cones for each team, placed level with the 1st and 4th Bending Poles. A flag will be placed in the holder nearer the changeover end.

Numbers One & Three will be at the Start/Finish end with Numbers Two & Four at the changeover end.

On the signal to start, Number One, carrying a flag, rides to the first Flag Cone and places the flag in it. They then ride to the second Flag Cone, takes the flag out and hands it to Number Two behind the Changeover line. Numbers Two, Three & Four will repeat the race in the same way up or down the arena.

Flag Cones knocked over must be set up immediately by the rider concerned.

Should a flag come off the cane, the cane alone may be used to complete the race.

The winning team is the one whose Number Four is first over the Finish Line carrying the flag.

27.   JUNIOR AREA GAMES 2024

EVENT 1: Bending

The details of this game are set out in Prince Philip Cup (Senior) Area Games, Event number 1.

EVENT 2: Equestrian Games 2 Mug

Four Bending Poles are placed in a line 7 to 9 metres apart. Mugs are placed on poles 1 and 3.

Numbers One and Three are mounted at the Start/Finish Line, Numbers Two and Four at the Changeover end.

On the signal to start Number One moves the Mug from Pole 1 to Pole 2, and the Mug from Pole 3 to Pole 4 and then rides across the Changeover Line.

Number Two moves the Mug from Pole 4 to Pole 3, and the Mug from Pole 2 to Pole 1 and then crosses the Start/Finish Line. Number Three repeats the actions of Number One and Number Four repeats the actions of Number Two.

The winning team is the one whose Number 4 crosses the Start/Finish Line first.

Mugs must be placed on each Pole in the correct order, should one fall or is missed the rider must replace the mug before continuing, if the next mug has already been moved then the rider must replace this mug on the correct pole before correcting the first error.

EVENT 3: Farmers' Market (Junior Version)

A table will be placed level with the first Bending Pole. Number Five stands behind a table placed 3 metres behind the Changeover Line. On the table will be placed four items (1 string of sausages, 1 potato, 1 egg box, 1 bottle of milk).

All four riders line up behind the Start/Finish Line. On the signal to start, Number One, carrying a tack box tray, rides and places the tray on the first table. They ride to Number Five who hands them any one of the items. They then ride back and place the item in the tray before riding over the Start/Finish Line.

Number Two rides to Number Five, collects any item, returns to place it in the tray and crosses the Start/Finish Line.

Number Three repeats the actions of Number Two.

Number Four repeats the actions of Number Two and Three but after placing the final item into the tray they then pick up and carry the tray containing the 'shopping' over the line to finish.

The milk bottle must be placed upright in the tray but does not need to remain so once the tray has been collected by Number Four.

The sausages may hang out over the edge of the tray.

EVENT 4: Tyre

The details of this game are set out in Prince Philip Cup (Senior) Area Games, Event number 5.

EVENT 5: Hollywood Bowl Bottle (Junior Version)

The details of this game are set out in Prince Philip Cup (Senior) Area Games, Event number 6 using the junior size Bottles containing sand weighing 440 grams.

EVENT 6: Old Sock (Junior Version)

A Bending Pole topped with a dish containing four socks will be placed 3 metres behind the Changeover Line. On the Centre Line there will be a bucket, one for each team.

All four riders form up behind the Start/Finish Line.

On the signal to start, Number One, carrying a sock ride to their team's bucket and drops the sock into it. They then continue to the far end, collect a sock from the dish and return to the Start/Finish Line to hand it to Number Two.

Numbers Two, Three and Four will complete the course in the same way in succession, with Number Four dropping the last sock into the bucket on their way back.

The winning team will be the one whose Number Four is first over the Finish Line.

EVENT 7: 5 Flag

The details of this game are set out in Prince Philip Cup (Senior) Area Games, Event number 8.

SPARE: 2 Flag

The details of this game are set out in Prince Philip Cup (Senior) Area Games, Spare Event.

28.   PAIRS AREA GAMES 2024

EVENT 1: Bending (Pairs)

Five Bending Poles are placed in a line 7 to 9 metres apart. Both riders are mounted at the Start/Finish end.

On the signal to start, Number One, carrying a Baton, rides down and back through the Bending Poles. After crossing the Start/Finish Line they hand the Baton to Number Two. Number Two will similarly ride down and back through the Bending Poles.

The winning Pair will be the one whose Number Two crosses the Start/Finish Line first, mounted, carrying the Baton.

Knocked down Bending Poles must be replaced by the rider concerned, they must go back and resume the race from the point where the Bending Pole was knocked down: they can resume by bending either side of the position of the knocked down Bending Pole and not necessarily on the same bend as before.

Line Stewards will not signal unless the Bending Pole is broken or lying flat on the ground.

EVENT 2: Equestrian Games 2 Mug (Pairs)

Four Bending Poles are placed in a line 7 to 9 metres apart. Mugs are placed on the 1st and 3rd poles.

Number One is mounted at the Start/Finish end, Number Two at the Changeover end.

On the signal to start Number One moves the mug from pole 1 to pole 2, the mug from pole 3 to pole 4 and then rides across the Changeover Line.

Number Two moves the mug from pole 4 to pole 3, and the mug from pole 2 to pole 1 and then rides across the Finish Line.

EVENT 3: Farmers' Market (Pairs)

A table will be placed level with the first Bending Pole. 3 metres behind the Changeover Line each team will have four items (1 string of sausages,

1 potato, 1 egg box, 1 bottle of milk) placed within the circle on the ground. The bottle of milk will be placed upright.

Both riders line up behind the Start/Finish Line. On the signal to start, Number One, carrying a tack box tray, rides and places the tray on the table. They ride to the far end, dismount, pick up any item and remount, return to place the item in the tray, they then ride back to the far end and collect a second item and places it into the tray and across the Start/Finish Line.

Number Two repeats the actions of Number One but after placing the final item into the tray they then pick up and carry the tray containing the 'shopping' over the Finish Line.

The milk bottle must be placed upright in the tray but does not need to remain so once the tray has been collected by Number Two.

The sausages may hang out over the edge of the tray. The bottle of milk must remain upright whilst in the circle and when placed into the tray until collected by Number Two.

Items knocked out of the circle other than the bottle should be replaced by the Line Steward concerned.

EVENT 4: PG Sports Pyramid (Spell PGUK) (Pairs)

A table will be placed on the Centre Line and another 3 metres behind the Changeover Line.

On the latter table will be placed four plastic Cartons (un-stacked) each with a printed letter on each side. As you look from the Start/Finish Line they will be placed as follows.

'K' Front right

'U' Back Right

'G' Back Left

'P' Front Left

At the signal to start, Number One rides to the table behind the Changeover Line and collects the Carton with the letter 'K' which is then placed on the Centre Line Bin/Table. Number One then returns to the table behind the Changeover Line and collects the letter 'U' and stacks this upon the previous Carton placed on the Centre Line table and then crosses the Start/Finish Line.

Number Two rides to the Table behind the Changeover Line, and in a similar manner to Number One collects the Carton with the letter 'G' followed by the letter 'P' and stacks these upon the previous Carton placed on the Centre Line table.

The winning Pair is the one whose Number Two is first over the Finish Line with all four Cartons stacked on the Centre Line table spelling from the top PGUK.

After collecting a Carton, the rider may adjust the stack by hand or with the Carton before or after placing their Carton on the stack. If the table is knocked over, or a Carton falls, the rider concerned may dismount to replace them in any order on the top table at the Changeover end, the Cartons must be placed side by side but not on top of each other, at the table on the Centre Line the Cartons must be stacked upright and in the correct order.

Line Stewards will only board once the incorrect carton has been placed on the Centre Line table.

EVENT 5: Tyre (Pairs)

A motorcycle Tyre will be placed on the Centre Line. Each pair will form up behind the Start/Finish Line.

On the signal to start, Number One and Two will ride to the Tyre where Number One dismounts, hands their pony to Number Two, gets through the Tyre and remounts. Both riders then continue to cross the Changeover Line where the Pair will turn and ride back towards the Tyre. Number Two dismounts, hands their pony to Number One, gets through the Tyre and remounts.

The winning Pair will be the one which crosses the Finish Line first, mounted on their ponies.

The rider who is to lead the pony may take hold of the rein behind the Start/Finish Line or as they go down the arena. The pony must be led by the rein nearer the ridden pony and not by the bit ring or any other part of the bridle. The Tyre may not be touched until the pony has been correctly handed over. Riders are not allowed to run with the Tyre.

The Tyre must remain inside of Poles 2 and 3 and in the Pair's lane throughout the race. If the Tyre rolls or is dragged outside of Poles 2 and 3 in the Pair's lane, then the dismounted rider must retrieve it before resuming the race.

EVENT 6: Hollywood Bowl Bottle (Pairs)

There will be 2 tables for each Pair, one on the Centre Line and the other 3 metres beyond the Changeover Line. On the latter table there will be a plastic Bottle, weighted with 500 grams of sand.

Each rider is mounted at the Start /Finish end.

On the signal to start, Number One, carrying a Bottle, rides to the centre and places it upright on the table. They then ride to the far end pick up the Bottle from far table and return to hand it to Number Two behind the Start/ Finish Line.

Rider Number Two rides to the far end and places the Bottle upright on the table. They then return to the Centre Line to pick up the Bottle from the table and cross the Finish Line.

The winning Pair will be the one whose Number Two crosses the Finish Line first, mounted carrying the Bottle. A Bottle knocked over must be replaced UPRIGHT.

EVENT 7: Old Sock (Pairs)

At the Changeover end each Pair will have two socks sewn into balls about the size of a fist, placed on the ground in the circle 3 metres beyond the Changeover Line. Across the Centre will be a row of buckets, one for each pair.

Both riders form up behind the Start/Finish Line

On the signal to start, Number One, carrying a sock, rides to their pair's bucket and drops the sock into it. They ride to the Changeover end, dismount, pick up a sock, remount and return to the start to hand it to Number Two.

Numbers Two will complete the course in the same way in succession, with Number Two dropping the last sock into the bucket on their way back.

The winning pair will be the one whose Number Two is first over the Finish Line with three socks in the bucket.

Line Stewards may replace socks in the circle where possible.

EVENT 8: 5 Flag (Pairs)

A Flag Cone will be placed 3 metres behind the Changeover Line and another on the Centre Line. Each Pair will have five Flags on Canes. Four of these will be in the pairs Flag Cone on the Centre Line and one will be carried by Number One at the start.

On the signal to start Number One rides to the Changeover end of the arena and places the Flag they are carrying in the Flag Cone. They ride back and pick a Flag out of their Flag Cone on the Centre Line. They then ride back up the arena and place the Flag into the Changeover end Flag Cone. On their return they collect another Flag from the Centre Flag Cone and hand this Flag to Number Two behind the Start/Finish Line.

Number Two will complete the course in the same way so that, at the end, the Pair will have placed four Flags in the Flag Cone at the far end of the arena and Number Two finishes over the Finish Line mounted and carrying the fifth Flag.

Should the Flag Cone be knocked over, the rider must put it up again, replacing any Flags there may have been in it. Should a rider take more than one Flag from the Flag Cone, they must replace the surplus. They may dismount to correct mistakes.

If the Flag should come off the Cane, the stick may be used to complete the race.

On windy days rubber bands can be used to keep the Flags furled and prevent them blowing together.

SPARE: 2 Flag (Pairs)

There will be two Flag Cones for each pair, placed level with the 1st and 4th Bending Poles. A flag will be placed in the holder nearer the Changeover end.

Number One, carrying a flag, is mounted at the Start/Finish end and Number Two mounted at the Changeover end.

On the signal to start, Number One, carrying a flag, rides to the first Flag Cone and places the flag in it. They then ride to the second Flag Cone, take the flag out and hand it to Number Two behind the Changeover Line. Number Two will repeat the race the same way down the arena.

Flag Cones knocked over must be set up immediately by the rider concerned. Should a flag come off the cane, the cane alone may be used to complete the race.

The winning Pair is the one whose Number Two is first over the Finish Line carrying the flag.

29.   PRINCE PHILIP CUP ZONE GAMES 2024

EVENT 1: STRUK Postman's

Four Bending Poles are placed in a line 7 to 9 metres apart.

The Number Five of each team stands 3 metres behind the Changeover Line, dismounted and having four wooden letters (see Equipment)

All four riders are mounted at the Start/Finish end.

On the signal to start Number One, carrying a sack, rides through the Bending Poles and across the Changeover Line, where Number Five hands them a letter. Number One places the letter in the sack before re-crossing the Changeover Line. They then return through the Bending Poles to hand the sack to Number Two.

Numbers Two, Three and Four repeat the actions of Number One, each collecting a letter from Number Five.

The winning team is the one whose Number Four is first over the Finish Line with four letters in the sack.

In all cases the letter must be placed in the sack and the rider's hand out of the sack before the rider crosses back into the field of play. Number Five is permitted to hold the pony whilst the letter is put in the sack by the rider, throughout the race they must remain behind the Changeover Line.

EVENT 2: Ball & Bucket

At the Changeover end each team will have four tennis balls placed on the ground in the circle 3 metres beyond the Changeover Line. Across the Centre will be a row of buckets, one for each team.

All four riders form up behind the Start/Finish Line.

On the signal to start, Number One carrying a tennis ball, rides to their team's bucket and drops the tennis ball into it. They ride towards the Changeover Line, dismount, pick up a tennis ball, remount and return to the start to hand it to Number Two.

Numbers Two, Three & Four will complete the course in the same way in succession, with Number Four dropping the last tennis ball into the bucket on their way back.

The winning team will be the one whose Number Four is first over the Finish Line with five tennis balls in the bucket.

Tennis balls knocked out of the circle should be replaced by the Line Steward concerned.

EVENT 3: Hollywood Bowl Bowling

FOUR full-sized Bottles weighted with 500 grams of sand will be placed 30 centimetres apart 3 metres beyond the Changeover Line

A Bucket with 12 weighted, plastic "Boules" will be placed in front of the Changeover Line.

All four riders are un-mounted at the Start/Finish end with two ponies.

Numbers One and Two will form up, on foot, behind the Start/Finish Line with one pony, each facing forward and on the same side. On the signal to start, Number One mounts the pony, before crossing the Start/Finish Line. Number Two then leads the pony across the Centre Line and waits whilst holding the pony. Number One dismounts after the Centre Line.

Whilst Number Two holds the pony, Number One runs to the Bucket and from behind the Changeover Line bowls/throws a Boule at the Bottles. They must knock down only one Bottle. (If they knock down more than the one Bottle, Number One must reset any others upright) Number One runs to the pony and whilst Number One holds the pony, Number Two runs to the Bucket and from behind the Changeover Line bowls/throws a Boule to knock down another Bottle (If they knock down more than the one Bottle, number two must reset any others upright). They then run back to the pony and Number Two mounts and Number 1 leads and runs with the pony before crossing the Centre Line. The riders then ride/run back over the Start/Finish Line.

Riders Numbers Three and Four repeat the actions of Numbers One and Two.

The winning team is the one whose Number Four riding and Number Three running are first over the Finish Line.

If a team completely runs out of Boules, the rider concerned must run forward with the Bucket to collect any number and then continue the race from behind the Changeover Line as before.

Ponies must be led by the nearer rein throughout. The white hat band is worn by the Number Four rider who is on the pony when crossing the Finish Line.

When bowling/throwing the Boules, the rider's foot must not be touching the line. Line Stewards will move forward and level with the changeover line and call 'Fault, throw again' if the rider's foot touches the line.

EVENT 4: Small Sack

Numbers One and Three will be mounted behind the Start/Finish Line, and Numbers Two and Four behind the Changeover Line.

On the signal to start Number One carrying a sack will ride forward, dismount and get into the sack before crossing the Centre Line. They run/jump across the Changeover Line, leading their pony to get out of the sack and hand it to Number Two. The rider must cross the Changeover Line but not necessarily the pony as well.

Number Two, Three and Four will complete the course in the same way up and down the arena in succession.

The winning team will be the one whose Number Four is first over the Finish Line.

Getting out of the sack and handing over must be done beyond the Changeover or Start/Finish Line.

Riders must not attempt to get into the sack until they have dismounted, nor may the top of the sack be rolled down. Every effort should be made to hold the sack above knee level throughout.

Riders must be on their feet when crossing the line, and the ponies must be led by the nearer rein only.

EVENT 5: Farmers Market

The details of this game are set out in Prince Philip Cup (Senior) Area Games, Event number 3.

EVENT 6: PG Sports Rosette Row

On the Centre Line there is a litter bin containing four coloured rosettes (each one has a large letter in the centre of it) with rings in a square formation:

Blue (letter P) at 12 o'clock

Red (letter G) at 3 o'clock

Green (U) at 6 o'clock

Yellow (K) at 9 o'clock

Number 5 stands 3 metres behind the Changeover Line facing down the arena, holding a gibbet with the hooks facing sideways and open to the right.

All four riders form up at the Start/Finish end. Number One has a cane with a small hook on one end.

On the signal to start. Number One rides to the litter bin, hooks ANY rosette, and continues over the Changeover Line to Number Five. Number Five unhooks the rosette and secures it on the gibbet hook in the correct order which will look to Number Five from left to the right: Yellow letter K, Green letter U, Red letter G, Blue letter P.

From the start line looking up the arena it will spell from left to right:

Blue 'P', Red 'G', Green 'U', Yellow 'K' - P G U K

Number One must remain behind the Changeover line until Number Five has correctly placed the rosette on the hook, they then return to the Start/ Finish Line and hand the cane to Number Two. If the rosette is placed on the wrong hook, this can be corrected if the rider comes back over the Changeover Line while Number Five corrects it.

Numbers Two, Three & Four complete the course in the same way.

The winning team is the one whose Number Four is first across the Finish Line with all four rosettes on the gibbet in the correct order. Should a rider drop a rosette, they may pick it up either mounted or dismounted, before replacing it on the hook of the cane. If a rosette is dropped whilst handing over to Number Five, the Number Five may pick it up and put it on the gibbet (See General Rules).

The rosette should be always on the hook when riding up the arena, however the cane will have a rubber stopper 10 centimetres from the hook to stop the rosette when hooked from travelling up the cane. Should the rosette go to the rubber stopper (not pass the rubber stopper) then the rider needs to stop and get the rosette back onto the hook before proceeding.

EVENT 7: Tyre

The details of this game are set out in Prince Philip Cup (Senior) Area Games, Event number 5.

EVENT 8: Ball & Racquet

A line of four Bending Poles is placed 7 to 9 metres apart.

Each team has a tennis racquet and ball.

Numbers One and Three are at the Start/Finish end with Number Two and Four at the Changeover end.

On the signal to start, Number One, carrying the tennis ball on the racquet, rides up the arena through the line of Bending Poles. They then hand the racquet to Number Two behind the Changeover Line.

Number Two repeats the process handing over to Number Three behind the Start/Finish Line.

Numbers Three and Four repeat the actions of Number One and Two respectively.

Each racquet has a crosspiece through the centre of the handle and the rider's hand must always be behind the crosspiece during the race and at the changeover.

EVENT 9: Stepping Stones

6 Stepping Stones are placed centrally, 30 centimetres apart in a straight line up and down the arena between the lines of Bending Poles. Numbers One and Three are mounted at the Start/Finish Line and Numbers Two and Four are mounted at the Changeover end.

On the signal to start Number One rides to the Stepping Stones, dismounts and leading their pony steps on each stone and then the ground with the opposite foot from the one used to step on the final stone before remounting to cross the line. Numbers Two, Three and Four will similarly complete the course up or down the arena in succession.

Should any pony or rider knock over a Stepping Stone or should a rider step on the ground crossing the Stepping Stones, they must set up the fallen stones and, in both cases, return to cross all the Stepping Stones again from the original direction they first attempted.

When dismounted, riders must lead the pony by the nearer rein throughout.

EVENT 10: Equestrian Games Tubular Flag Race

A 4 Flag Holder is placed 3 metres behind the Changeover Line and 4 White Flags are placed in a Flag Cone on the Centre Line. The 4 Flag Holder when looking from the Start/Finish Line should have the white tubes at 12, 4 & 8 o'clock.

All four riders are mounted at the Start/Finish Line.

On the signal to start Number One carrying the BLUE EGUK LOGO FLAG rides to the far end of the arena and places the Flag in the CENTRE matching blue tube. This must be done from the mounted position. They then ride back picking up a Flag out of the Centre Line Flag Cone and hand it to Number Two behind the Start/Finish Line.

Numbers Two, Three and Four complete the course in the same way matching their White Flags to any of the remaining tubes in succession so that at the end, the team has placed four Flags in the 4 Flag Holder correctly.

The winning team is the one whose Number Four finishes first over the Start/Finish Line carrying the 5th Flag.

If a rider successfully places their flag into the 4 Flag Holder and then knocks over the holder, they may replace all flags back into the holder from the ground:

The 4 Flag Holder. An array of four tubes, the central one BLUE, the other 3 tubes WHITE equally spaced clockwise around it. Each tube is between 20 cm and 30 cm long, made of plastic with an internal diameter of 2.3cms and an external diameter of 3 cm. The tubes are set in a weighted conical base of about 4kg which has no sharp edges or corners and a diameter of about 26cm at the base (same as Pony Club knock down bending poles bases used on arenas).

NB. For external shows and competitions PROVIDED THAT the first Flag is of a different colour from the other Flags, is placed in the centre tube and remains there, there is no need to use a blue Flag to start with or 4 whites Flags to follow. The Chief Steward should state what colour Flags are going to be used before the competition starts.

SPARE: 2 Flag

The details of this game are set out in Prince Philip Cup (Senior) Area Games, Spare Event.

30.   JUNIOR ZONE GAMES 2024

EVENT 1: STRUK Bending

The details of this game are set out in Prince Philip Cup (Senior) Area Games, Event number 1.

EVENT 2: Old Sock

The details of this game are set out in Prince Philip Cup (Senior) Area Games, Event number 7.

EVENT 3: Hollywood Bowl Bowling (Junior Version)

FOUR full-sized Bottles weighted with 500 grams of sand will be placed 30 centimetres apart 3 metres beyond the Changeover Line.

A Bucket with 12 weighted, plastic "Boules" will be placed in front of the Changeover Line.

Two riders are mounted with two riders un-mounted at the Start/Finish end with two ponies only. Numbers Three and Four are behind the 6 metre Line at the start. Number Two holding the pony by the rein in their right hand behind the Start/Finish Line with one pony with Number One mounted on the pony. Number Two then leads the pony across the Centre Line and waits whilst holding the pony. Number One dismounts after the Centre Line.

Whilst Number Two holds the pony, Number One runs to the Bucket and from behind the Changeover Line bowls/throws a Boule at the Bottles. They must knock down only one Bottle. (If they knock down more than the one Bottle, Number One must reset any others upright) Number One runs to the pony and whilst Number One holds the pony, Number Two runs to the Bucket and from behind the Changeover Line bowls/throws a Boule to knock down another Bottle (If they knock down more than the one Bottle, Number Two must reset any others upright)

They then run back to the pony and Number Two mounts, and Number One leads and runs with the pony before crossing the Centre Line. The riders then ride/run back over the Start/Finish Line.

Riders Numbers Three and Four repeat the actions of Numbers One and Two.

The winning team is the one whose Numbers Four riding and Number Three running are first over the Finish Line.

If a team completely runs out of Boules, the rider concerned must run forward with the Bucket to collect any number and then continue the race from behind the Changeover Line as before.

Ponies must be led by the nearer rein throughout. The white hat band is worn by the Number Four rider who is on the pony when crossing the Finish Line.

When bowling/throwing the Boules, the rider's foot must not be touching the line. Line Stewards will move forward and level with the Changeover Line and call 'Fault, throw again' if the rider's foot touches the line.

EVENT 4: Small Sack (Junior Version)

A table will be placed 3 metres behind the Changeover line. A table will be placed 1 metre from the Centre Line (on the Changeover side).

Riders Number One and Three will be at the Start/Finish end and Numbers Two and Four without their ponies at the Changeover end.

On the signal to Start Number One carrying the sack rides to and drops the sack in the bin – they then continue to the Changeover Line where Number Two is waiting behind the bin. When Number One has crossed the Changeover Line Number Two runs to the sack, steps in it before crossing the Centre Line and then runs/jumps to the Start/Finish Line where they hand the sack to Number Three.

Number Three repeats the action of Number One. Number Four repeats the action of Number Two. The winner will be the one whose Number Four is completely over the Finish Line with their feet in the sack.

Sacks must be completely in the bin and not showing.

EVENT 5: Farmers' Market (Junior Version)

The details of this game are set out in Prince Philip Cup (Junior) Area Games, Event number 3.

EVENT 6: PG Sports Rosette Row (Junior Version)

On the Centre Line there is a table with four coloured rosettes (each one has a large letter in the centre of it) with hooks on. Each rosette is placed individually on top of each other in the following order:

Yellow rosette (letter K) is placed up and down with the ring at 6 o'clock, Green rosette (letter U) is placed side to side with the ring at 9 o'clock, Red rosette (letter G) is placed up and down with the ring at 6 o'clock and the Blue rosette (letter P) is placed side to side with the ring at 9 o'clock.

Number Five stands 3 metres behind the Changeover Line facing down the arena, holding a gibbet with hooks facing sideways and open to the right.

All four riders form up at the Start/Finish end.

On the signal to start, Number One rides to the table and picks up one rosette and continues over the Changeover Line to Number Five. Number Five is handed the rosette and secures it on the gibbet hook in the correct order which will look to Number Five from left to right:

Yellow letter K, Green letter U, Red letter G, Blue letter P

From the Start/Finish line looking up the arena it will spell from left to right:

Blue 'P', Red' G', Green 'U', Yellow 'K' - P G U K

Number One must remain behind the Changeover Line until Number Five has correctly placed the rosette on the correct hook, they then return to the Start/Finish Line. If the rosette is placed on the wrong hook, this can be corrected if the rider comes back over the Changeover Line while Number Five corrects it.

Numbers Two, Three & Four each in turn complete the course in the same way.

The winning team is the one whose Number Four is first across the Finish Line with all four rosettes on the gibbet in the correct order. Should a rider drop a rosette, they may dismount and pick it up before continuing. If a rosette is dropped whilst handing over to Number Five, the Number Five may pick it up and put it on the gibbet (See General Rules). Should a rider knock off any rosettes from the table at the Centre Line, these can be replaced in any order.

EVENT 7: Tyre

The details of this game are set out in Prince Philip Cup (Senior) Area Games, Event number 5.

EVENT 8: Equestrian Games Tubular Flag Race

The details of this game are set out in Prince Philip Cup (Senior) Zone Games, Event number 10.

SPARE: 2 Flag

The details of this game are set out in Prince Philip Cup (Senior) Area Games, Spare Event.

31.   PAIRS ZONE GAMES 2024

EVENT 1: STRUK Bending (Pairs)

The details of this game are set out in Pairs Area Games Event number 1.

EVENT 2: Ball & Bucket (Pairs)

At the Changeover end each Pair will have two tennis balls placed on the ground in the circle 3 metres beyond the Changeover Line. Across the Centre will be a row of buckets, one for each pair.

Both riders form up behind the Start/Finish Line.

On the signal to start, Number One, carrying a tennis ball, rides to their pair's bucket and drops the tennis ball into it. They ride to the Changeover end, dismount, pick up a tennis ball, remount and return to the Start/Finish end to hand it to Number Two.

Numbers Two will complete the course in the same way in succession, with Number Two dropping the last tennis ball into the bucket on their way back.

The winning pair will be the one whose Number Two is first over the Finish Line with three tennis balls in the bucket.

Line Stewards may replace tennis balls in the circle where possible.

EVENT 3: Hollywood Bowl Bowling (Pairs)

Four full-sized, weighted Bottles with 500 grams in each will be placed 30 centimetres apart 3 metres beyond the Changeover Line.

A Bucket with 12 weighted, plastic "Boules" will be placed in front of the Changeover Line.

Both riders are mounted at the Start/Finish end.

At the signal to start, both will ride down the arena and across the Centre Line where both riders dismount.

Whilst one rider holds both ponies, the other rider runs to the bucket and from behind the Changeover Line bowls/throws a Boule at two Bottles. They must knock down two Bottles, even if this is done using just one Boule. They then run back and hold both ponies whilst the other rider takes their turn to bowl/throw to knock down the remaining two Bottles The second thrower returns to their pony and both re-mount before crossing the Centre Line. Both riders then ride back over the Finish Line. Should the first thrower knock down more than two Bottles they must stand the others upright before returning to hold both ponies.

If a Pair completely runs out of Boules, the rider concerned must run forward with the Bucket to collect any number of Boules and then continue the race from behind the Changeover Line as before.

Ponies must be led by the nearer rein throughout. The white hat band is worn by the rider who throws the last Boule.

When bowling/throwing the Boules, the rider's foot must not be touching the line. Line Stewards will move forward and level with the changeover line and call 'Fault, throw again' if the rider's foot touches the line.

EVENT 4: Small Sack (Pairs)

Number One will be mounted behind the Start/Finish Line, and Number Two behind the Changeover Line.

On the signal to start Number One carrying a Sack will ride forward, dismount, and get into the Sack before crossing the Centre Line. They run or hop to the end of the arena, leading their pony, get out of the Sack and hand it to Number Two. Number One in their sack must cross the Changeover Line but not necessarily the pony as well. Getting out of the Sack and handing it over must be done beyond the Changeover Line.

Number Two will complete the course the same way before crossing the Start/Finish Line on their feet in the Sack and leading their pony.

Riders must not attempt to get into the Sack until they have dismounted, nor may the top of the Sack be rolled down. Every effort should be made to hold the Sack above knee level throughout.

Riders must be on their feet when crossing the line, and the ponies must be led by the nearer rein only.

The winning Pair will be the one whose Number Two is first across the Finish Line, on their feet, in the Sack, leading their pony.

EVENT 5: Farmers' Market (Pairs)

The details of this game are set out in Pairs Area Games, Event number 3.

EVENT 6: PG Sports Pyramid (Pairs)

The details of this game are set out in Pairs Area Games Event number 4.

EVENT 7: Tyre (Pairs)

The details of this game are set out in Pairs Area Games Event number 5.

EVENT 8: Ball & Racquet (Pairs)

A line of four Bending Poles is placed 7 to 9 metres apart.

Each pair has a tennis racquet and ball.

Numbers One is at the Start/Finish end with Number Two at the Changeover end.

On the signal to start, Number One, carrying the tennis ball on the racquet, rides up the arena through the line of Bending Poles. They then hand the racquet to Number Two behind the Changeover Line.

Number Two repeats the process and crosses the Finish Line.

Each racquet has a crosspiece through the centre of the handle and the rider's hand must always be behind the crosspiece during the race and at the Changeover.

EVENT 9: Stepping Stones (Pairs)

6 Stepping Stones are placed centrally, 30 centimetres apart in a straight line up and down the arena between the lines of Bending Poles.

Number One is mounted at the Start/Finish end of the arena and Number Two is mounted at the Changeover end.

On the signal to start Number One rides to the Stepping Stones, dismounts and leading their pony steps on each Stepping Stone and then the ground with the opposite foot from the one used to step on the final Stepping Stone before remounting to cross the Changeover Line.

Number Two will similarly complete the course down the arena and cross the Finish Line.

Should any pony or rider knock over a Stepping Stone or should a rider step on the ground crossing the stones, they must set up the fallen stones and, in both cases, return to cross all the Stepping Stones again, in the direction they were travelling, even if it is the last one which has fallen.

EVENT 10: Equestrian Games Tubular Flag Race (Pairs)

A 4 Flag Holder is placed 3 metres behind the Changeover Line and 4 White Flags are placed in a Flag Cone on the Centre Line. The 4 Flag Holder when looking from the Start/Finish Line should have the white tubes at 12, 4 & 8 o'clock.

Both riders are mounted at the Start/Finish Line.

On the signal to start Number One carrying the BLUE EGUK LOGO FLAG rides to the far end of the arena and places the Flag in the CENTRE matching blue tube - this must be done from the mounted position. Number One then rides back and collects a second Flag from the Centre Line Flag Cone and rides back up the arena and places the Flag into one of the other tubes, Number One then collects another Flag from the Flag Cone on the Centre Line and hands it to Number Two behind the Start/Finish Line.

Number Two completes the course in the same way matching their White Flags to any of the remaining tubes in succession so that at the end, the Pair has placed four Flags in the Flag Holder correctly.

The winning Pair is the one whose Number Two finishes first over the Finish Line carrying the 5th Flag.

If a rider successfully places their flag into the 4 Flag Holder and then knocks over the holder, they may replace all flags back into the holder from the ground.

NB. For external shows and competitions PROVIDED THAT the first Flag is of a different colour from the other Flags, is placed in the centre tube and remains there, there is no need to use a blue Flag to start with or 4 white flags.

Flags to follow. The Chief Steward should state what colour Flags are going to be used before the competition starts.

SPARE: 2 Flag (Pairs)

The details of this game are set out in Pairs Area Games Spare Event.

APPENDICES

APPENDIX A – PLAN OF ARENA

1.　　　Arena Size – including collecting ring 125m X 74m

2.　　　Manned ropes should be used to open and close the entrance and exit at the start and finish of each race.

3.　　　In games where equipment or the fifth member is positioned 3m beyond the Changeover line, a circle (45cm diameter) should be marked on the ground.

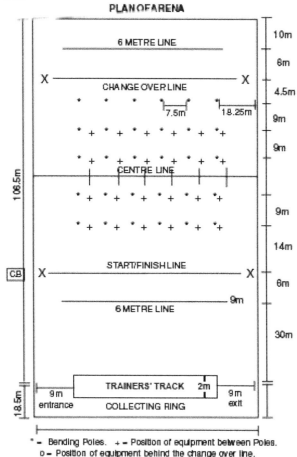

PLAN OF ARENA

* − Bending Poles. 　+ − Position of equipment between Poles.
　o − Position of equipment behind the change over line.

KEY

CB Commentator's Box　　***** Bending Posts　　**X** Corner marker posts
+ Centre of lane markers for non-bending events

APPENDIX B – MOUNTED GAMES EQUIPMENT – ALPHABETICAL

Recommended items of equipment for Area and Zone Competitions (All sizes are approximate).

Quantities are for 6 teams in heats or finals.

These are the minimum requirements and spares should be available in case of loss or breakage.

Ball & Bucket

- 30 Tennis Balls
- 6 Buckets

Ball & Bucket (Pairs)

- 18 Tennis Balls
- 6 Buckets

Ball & Racquet

- 24 Bending Poles
- 6 Tennis Balls
- 6 Tennis racquets wooden or plastic with crosspiece 13mm in diameter through handle

Bending

- 30 Bending Poles, plus some spares. Poles should be approx. 3cm in diameter and not more than 3.5cm diameter, 1.4m long.
- 6 Batons, 2.5cm in diameter and 30cm long

Equestrian Games 2 Mug

- 24 Bending Poles
- 12 Mugs

Equestrian Games 5 Mug

- 30 Bending Poles
- 30 Mugs including 6 with the EGUK logo on
- 6 Tables

Equestrian Games Tubular Flag Race

- 6 Four Flag Holders
- 6 Blue Flags

- ▸ 24 White Flags
- ▸ 6 Flag Cones

Farmers' Market

- ▸ 6 Tables
- ▸ 6 Plastic Tack Box Trays
- ▸ 6 Strings of Sausages (tights knotted to make 6 x 10cm sausages)
- ▸ 6 Senior size Bottles (filled with 500 grams of sand)
- ▸ 6 Brown Socks (rolled fist sized) weighing 100-150g (Potatoes)
- ▸ 6 Egg Boxes x 6 (with 500 grams of sand and securely taped)

Farmers' Market (JV)

- ▸ 12 Tables
- ▸ 6 Plastic Tack Box Trays
- ▸ 6 Strings of Sausages (tights knotted to make 6 x 10cm sausages)
- ▸ 6 Junior size Bottles (filled with 440 grams of sand)
- ▸ 6 Brown Socks (rolled fist sized) weighing 100-150g (Potatoes)
- ▸ 6 Egg Boxes x 6 (with 500 grams of sand and securely taped)

5 Flag

- ▸ 30 Flags (1.25m long), consisting of good quality bamboo or plastic canes with flags firmly fixed. Flags to be 23cm square or 23cm triangle)
- ▸ 12 Flag Cones (flag holders with the tops cut off to leave a hole 10cm diameter)

Hollywood Bowl Bottle

- ▸ 12 Tables
- ▸ 12 Senior size Bottles (filled with 500 grams of sand)

Hollywood Bowl Bottle (JV)

- ▸ 12 Tables
- ▸ 12 Junior size Bottles (filled with 440 grams of sand)

Hollywood Bowl Bowling Race

- ▸ 6 Pink Buckets
- ▸ 24 Bottles (Senior size weighing 500g)
- ▸ 72 Boules

Old Sock

- ▸ 30 Socks (rolled fist sized)
- ▸ 6 Buckets

Old Sock (JV)

- ▸ 30 Socks (rolled fist sized)
- ▸ 6 Buckets
- ▸ 6 Penny Trays

Old Sock (Pairs)

- ▸ 18 Socks (rolled fist sized)
- ▸ 6 Buckets

PG Sports Pyramid (spell PGUK)

- ▸ 12 Tables
- ▸ 6 Cartons with the letter 'P' on each side
- ▸ 6 Cartons with the letter 'G' on each side
- ▸ 6 Cartons with the letter 'U' on each side
- ▸ 6 Cartons with the letter 'K' on each side

PG Sports Rosette Row

- ▸ 6 Bins
- ▸ 6 Gibbets
- ▸ 6 Canes with a hook and a stopper 10 centimetres from the hook
- ▸ 6 Blue Plastic Rosettes with the letter 'P' on each side
- ▸ 6 Red Plastic Rosettes with the letter 'G' on each side
- ▸ 6 Green Plastic Rosettes with the letter 'U' on each side
- ▸ 6 Yellow Plastic Rosettes with the letter 'K' on each side

PG Sports Rosette Row (JV)

- ▸ 6 Tables
- ▸ 6 Gibbets
- ▸ 6 Blue Plastic Rosettes with the letter 'P' on each side
- ▸ 6 Red Plastic Rosettes with the letter 'G' on each side
- ▸ 6 Green Plastic Rosettes with the letter 'U' on each side
- ▸ 6 Yellow Plastic Rosettes with the letter 'K' on each side

Small Sack

- ▸ 6 small sacks - Hessian sacks 63.5kg capacity

Small Sack (JV)

- ▸ 6 small sacks - Hessian sacks 63.5kg capacity
- ▸ 6 Bins

Stepping Stones

- 36 Stepping Stones

STRUK Bending

- 30 Bending Poles, plus some spares. Poles should be approx. 3cm in diameter and not more than 3.5cm diameter, 1.4m long.
- 6 Batons, 2.5cm in diameter and 30cm long

STRUK Postman's

- 24 Bending Poles
- 6 Postman's Sacks - 51cm deep x 38cm wide
- 24 Letters - each 20cm x 10cm with rounded corners

2 Flag

- 12 Flags
- 12 Flag Cones

Tyre

- 6 Motorcycle Tyres - 7cm X 45cm (approximately)

STARTER'S FLAG

1 White Flag approximately 30cm x 30cm, on a cane.

LINE STEWARD BOARDS

12 Square boards, numbered in pairs 1-6 measuring 20cm x 20cm with a narrow piece attached to the back measuring 50cm (with 20cm over hanging forming the handle) – see below.

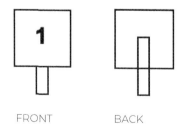

FRONT   BACK

SWEATERS

Wainwright Screenprint, Middle Street, Dewlish, Dorchester, Dorset, DT2 7LX can supply white V-neck sweaters suitable for use at Mounted Games

Competitions. They can also produce Pony Club or Branch logos on these sweaters. Tel: 01258 837364, www.wainwrightscreenprint.co.uk, info@wainwrightscreenprint.co.uk

APPENDIX C – DIRECTIONS FOR ORGANISERS

ADMINISTRATION

It is essential that Organisers should have a thorough knowledge of the whole Contents of this Rule Book.

LINE STEWARDS – AREA COMPETITIONS

The names and addresses of Nominated Line Stewards will be sent by Branches/Centres to the Organiser or Line Steward Co-ordinators (if appointed) before the Competition as requested.

Organisers should provide a list of Line Stewards for the Official Steward before the Briefing.

Close liaison with the Area Line Steward Co-ordinator (if appointed) or Organiser is essential.

ORGANISERS – LINE STEWARD CO-ORDINATORS (IF APPOINTED)

Each Organiser or Area Line Steward Co-ordinator (if appointed) will attempt to find and appoint at least six experienced and independent Line Stewards for his Area Meeting.

Organisers and Line Steward Co-ordinators must consult and agree how many of the Branch/Centre nominees are required.

Those nominees not needed must be informed in good time.

TEAM COLOURS

Each team at Area Meetings will wear their Branch/Centre colours.

LAYOUT OF SHOWGROUND

The size of the Arena is 125 m x 74m (SEE APPENDIX A).

There will be a "6m line" behind the Start and Changeover lines.

It is possible for about six people to mark out the Arena and put up all the arena posts, ropes and equipment in a morning. Metal posts must not be used.

The other requirements are:

- ▸ First Aid Cover
- ▸ Signposting on the roads

- ►   Horsebox Park
- ►   Water must be available
- ►   Secretary's Tent (Horsebox or trailer)
- ►   Public Address System
- ►   Scoreboard
- ►   Ladies' and Gentlemen's Toilets
- ►   Commentator's Box
- ►   Public Refreshment Outlet
- ►   An area for Judges/Officials to take lunch (usually provided by the Organiser)
- ►   The Commentator's Box should be approximately in line with the Start/Finish Line
- ►   The Public Address Equipment must be tested and in action before the start of the first event

TECHNICAL EQUIPMENT

If Organisers already have some different, but equally suitable, equipment, this may be used, but teams must be given details at least one month before the competition so that they can practise accordingly.

SPONSORSHIP

Sponsors at Area Competitions must not be competitors of the main sponsors of the discipline, and must be approved by The Pony Club office. Any advertising material that is used by sponsors, whether it be in the form of display banners or programme material, must be tasteful, and not inappropriate to the image of The Pony Club.

PROGRAMME

The minimum requirements in the Programme are:

- ►   A list of Events
- ►   A Timetable
- ►   The Teams taking part and their colours
- ►   A Score Sheet
- ►   The names of the Organiser and Official Steward

BRIEFING

The Briefing is carried out by the Official Steward.

It should be held not later than one hour before the start of the first event. It is strongly recommended that arrangements are made for the Briefing to be held under cover if the weather is likely to be inclement.

Those required at the Briefing are:

Official Steward, District Commissioners, Team Trainer, Both Judges, Starter, All Line Stewards and Line Steward Co-ordinator (if appointed).

If the Briefing takes place at the same time as the Turnout Inspection, Team Trainers must nominate a substitute to attend their Team's inspection.

SECRETARY

The Secretary is responsible for Programmes, Rosettes and Catering arrangements.

The Secretary receives the Declaration Forms and gives them to the Official Steward for checking before the Briefing.

FIRST AID REQUIREMENTS

PLEASE SEE THE HEALTH AND SAFETY RULE BOOK OR PCUK.ORG

VETERINARY SURGEON

If a veterinary surgeon cannot attend, arrangements must be made for them to be 'on call' and able to attend the site in a reasonable time. The telephone number should be noted in the Secretary's Tent.

The Veterinary Surgeon and medical personnel and the Ambulance are best situated near the ring.

A tarpaulin should be available to cover a pony should one be killed, and the telephone number of the Hunt Kennels noted in the Secretary's Tent. See the Health and Safety Rule Book for further information.

FARRIER

If possible, the Organiser should arrange for a Farrier to be present or on call.

GATE STEWARD

They direct the parking of vehicles.

PROGRAMME SELLERS

Programme Sellers (if used) should be arranged by the Organiser.

One may be positioned near the gate but not obstructing the entrance.

ROSETTES

Rosettes for Area Competitions are ordered and supplied by the Organiser of that competition. These are given for the final placings only and not for each separate event. Rosettes are awarded to the five riding team members and the sixth non-riding reserve.

- ► Up to 8 entries – 1st, 2nd, 3rd and 4th
- ► Up to 10 entries – 5th in addition
- ► Over 10 entries – 6th in addition

It is recommended that all Team Members receive a rosette.

At Zone and Championship Competitions, the five riding members and the sixth non-riding reserve from all teams will receive rosettes. These will be supplied by The Pony Club Office.

THE TURNOUT COMPETITION

All teams will be inspected before the start of the competition, in the clothing and saddlery in which they are to compete. See under INSPECTION (Rule 22 f). Branches/Centres must be notified in advance of the times when their teams will be inspected and it is strongly recommended that a time-table is worked out, at five-minute intervals, so that competitors do not have to stand about for long periods in inclement weather. Team Trainers or their nominee must be with their Team when inspected, see under BRIEFING.

All teams then parade before the start of the competition, see Initial Parade (Rule 22 g).

Rosettes will be ordered and awarded by the Organisers to the first three teams. The results of the Turnout Competition should be displayed on the scoreboard.

REPORT TO THE PONY CLUB OFFICE

Immediately after the Competition, the Organiser must give to the OFFICIAL STEWARD the following documents, which the OFFICIAL STEWARD must send by post or email to The Pony Club Office IMMEDIATELY:

- ► A copy of the Programme
- ► A Marked-Up Score Sheet for Prince Philip Cup, Junior and Pairs Team Competitions.
- ► Declaration Forms of All Teams
- ► A report on any difficulties that arose and suggestions for improvements for the future.

NOTICE TO TEAMS

The Organiser should inform the teams of the following:

    i.   The venue and directions how to get there.

    ii.   Times of:

        a.   Declarations

        b.   Briefing

        c.   Turnout Inspection

        d.   Start of First Event

    iii.   Description of technical equipment to be used if different from the list in APPENDIX B and the distance between Bending Posts, if not 9m.

    iv.   Whether catering facilities are provided.

    v.   The Organiser's details with telephone number and Mobile Contact Number on the day.

The Organiser must also inform the Official Steward of all the arrangements as soon as possible and seek his/her advice in case of any difficulties.

The Organiser/Line Steward Co-ordinator (if appointed) is responsible for the appointment of all Line Stewards.

APPENDIX D – THE OFFICIAL STEWARD – DUTIES

The Official Steward, who is appointed by The Pony Club Office, is responsible for ensuring that the whole competition is run in accordance with the rules. Their authority is final and binding. They are responsible for inspecting and approving the lay-out of the arena and all the equipment. They conduct the Briefing (after calling the roll). See Briefing, APPENDIX E. They supervise the Line Stewards and allocates where they should stand. They appoint an experienced Line Steward on the far side of the arena to receive any objections (on his behalf), they will emphasise that the Line Steward must immediately raise their board and not discuss the objection. They may replace a Line Steward if they consider it necessary. They receive reports on infringements and informs the Chief Judge of their decisions.

The Official Steward must liaise with the First Aid personnel and agree where they should be positioned during the Competition and when they should be summoned.

They are responsible for the enforcement of the Rule about Concussion (PLEASE SEE THE HEALTH AND SAFETY RULE BOOK or pcuk.org)

They adjudicate on objections. If unable to give a decision on the day, they may refer the matter to The Pony Club Office for adjudication.

If, because of any serious breach of the rules, the Official Steward considers disqualification from the whole competition may be necessary, they can consult with the Organiser and any member of the Mounted Games Committee present before taking their decision. They will report the matter to The Pony Club Office

The Official Steward shall adjudicate on any unforeseen eventualities.

They must have available a height-measuring stick and scales (bathroom scales are adequate). They must have a whistle immediately available in case it is necessary to stop a race. They thank the Organiser on behalf of the Mounted Games Committee at the end of the day.

Immediately after the Competition, the OFFICIAL STEWARD must send to The Pony Club Office:

- ▸ A copy of the Programme
- ▸ A marked-Up Score Sheet (FOR PRINCE PHILIP CUP, JUNIOR AND PAIRS TEAM COMPETITIONS)
- ▸ Declaration Forms of All Teams
- ▸ A report on any difficulties that arose and suggestions for improvements for the future

APPENDIX E – BRIEFING

The Briefing is conducted by the Official Steward. It should take place not less than one hour before the start of the first event, preferably under cover. Punctual attendance at the Briefing is essential by all concerned.

The Organiser should hand all Declaration Forms to the Official Steward for verification before the start of the Briefing.

The Organiser also provides for the Official Steward a list of Line Stewards. Before the Briefing begins, the Official Steward should call the roll to ensure that everyone is present. Those required are:

- District Commissioners / Centre Proprietors, or their officially appointed representatives
- Team Trainers
- All Line Stewards
- The Judges (2)
- The Starter
- Line Steward Co-ordinator (if appointed)

The Official Steward should ensure that all questions and all answers are heard by everyone present. They verify that all Line Stewards have read and understand their duties as set out in APPENDIX F.

They explain the Line Steward's signalling procedure and reminds them that they must NOT call back or warn any competitor.

They will appoint and brief an experienced Line Steward (on the far side of the arena) to receive any objections. They will emphasise that the Line Steward must, on receiving an objection, immediately raise their board and not discuss the objection.

To help the running of the competition they will remind the Line Stewards at the Start/Finish end to hand out any piece of equipment needed e.g. baton. Similarly, they will collect equipment in at the end of the race. Changeover Line Stewards will be responsible for equipment at the far end of the arena.

They explain the use of the Starter's whistle in the event of a false start. They remind Line Stewards that they must not steward their own team, and stresses the need for absolute concentration while the races are in progress.

They summarise the principal points in General Rules.

They run over any special points that require attention in each race.

Objections: The Official Steward should explain the rules regarding objections and explain that no objections of any kind are allowed to the starting, judging or stewarding of any race.

Before briefing the Judges and Starter, others present can be allowed to go. Judges: The Judges must be together at the same end of the start/finish line as the commentator for easy liaison.

The Judges place the competitors as they cross the finish line and they must not concern themselves with infringements. At Zone Finals and Championships, the Judges will liaise with the Official Steward on Start/Finish line infringements.

The Judges place all teams and record these places (in case of eliminations). The Official Steward should explain the finish of each race, see Rule 24(d).

Briefing Notes may be sent from the Official Steward/Organiser before the competition'

THE STARTER

Starter: The Official Steward should check with the Starter where they stand to signal the start and the correct use of their flag. The Starter's whistle must be immediately available in the event of a false start.

1. The person appointed should be experienced in starting Mounted Games competitions.

2. The Starter's position is in line with the first bending pole and on the same side as the Judges. They must ensure they can be clearly seen by all the competitors on the start line.

3. Should any pony become unruly at the start the Starter/Official Steward will order it to stand behind the 6m line.

4. In the event of a false start, the Starter will immediately blow their whistle and raise their flag to recall the teams.

5. As soon as the teams are assembled on the line the Starter should:

    i. Raise the flag and hold it upright whilst the riders settle; they should have the whistle ready in their other hand.
    ii. When they are satisfied all the riders are settled and stationary the flag is lowered AWAY FROM THE RIDERS. (There is no need to bring the flag down with a great flourish as this will invariably unsettle the pony in the nearest lane).
    iii. The practice of riders holding up their hand when they feel they

are not ready should be discouraged. The Starter should tell them they can see the situation and that they have better control with two hands on the reins.

6.   Should the Starter have any doubts he should consult the Official Steward for guidance.

APPENDIX F – INSTRUCTIONS FOR LINE STEWARDS AT AREA COMPETITIONS

1. The line steward signals are for the guidance of the Official Steward and not for the competitors.

2. Line Stewards must have a thorough knowledge of the rules and have studied carefully the details of each race in the competition they are to steward.

    It is most important that they have Line Stewarded at a minimum of two team practices/competitions, and preferably more, before the competition at which they are to Steward

    They must have attained their 18th birthday.

3. They must attend the Briefing, which is normally not less than one hour before the first event. Punctuality is essential.

4. a)   Each Team will have Two Line Stewards. IMPORTANT N.B.

    One Line Steward will stand 3-4m behind the Changeover line – in line with the lane they are judging.

    The Second Line Steward will stand at the side of the arena as instructed by the Official Steward.

    When Six Teams are running, lane 1, 2, 3 Line Stewards will stand on the starter's side and lane 4, 5, 6 Line Stewards will stand on the opposite side. They must stand apart and ensure they can see the changeovers.

    b)   Each Line Steward will have a numbered board; if possible, they should all wear a fluorescent bib for visibility.

5. Where possible Line Stewards should not act in a heat or final in which their own team is competing.

6. Any infringement of the rules must be signalled at once by raising the numbered board high, keeping it up until the end of the race, unless the infringement is corrected, when it is immediately lowered again.

7. When a Line Steward signals an infringement, the Line Steward at the opposite end should also signal immediately.

8. In the case of obstruction by any team, the Line Steward of the team causing the obstruction does NOT signal until the end of the race.

At that time the board is raised for the attention of the Official Steward who will then adjudicate. The Line Steward of the team obstructed does NOT signal.

9. Line Stewards must not call back or call instructions to any competitor, but the Changeover Line Steward must answer a competitor's question as briefly as possible.

10. Line Stewards at the Changeover Line should ensure that competitors do not ride back down the arena until the race is over.

11. If one team's equipment is upset by another team, the nearest Line Steward of the team upset should quickly set this up again, if this is possible and safe to do so.

12. Close concentration is necessary throughout each race. Be sure not to be distracted by anything – even a bad upset in another lane. Mobile phones must be switched off and not used by a line steward during the competition.

13. If equipment is broken and appears dangerous the Line Steward has the discretion to raise his board. The race will not be re-run.

   See General Rules.

14. Ensure that only the next rider to go takes up his position on the Start or Changeover Line. The others must be behind the 6m line. See General Rules.

15. If a pony runs loose, the Line Stewards of the team concerned may endeavour to catch it after it has left the 'playing area'.

16. Line Stewards are not responsible for the position of the ponies at the start.

17. Even if a Branch/Centre Team is withdrawn from the Competition, the Line Stewards from that Branch/Centre must still attend the Area Meeting unless otherwise notified by the Organiser.

18. Line Stewards will report to the Official Steward any person who questions their decisions, is abusive or obstructs their duties in any way whatsoever.

   Briefing Notes may be sent from the Official Steward/Organiser before the competition

APPENDIX G – HEAD INJURY AND CONCUSSION FLOWCHART

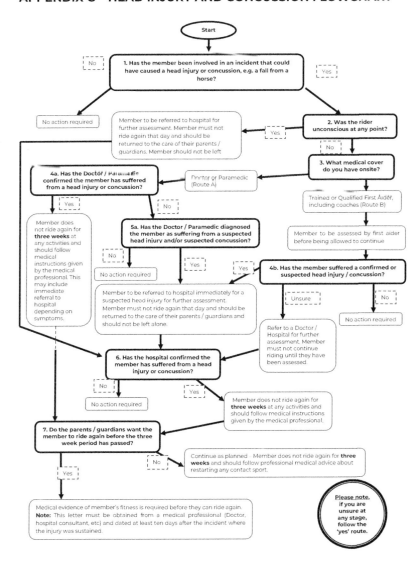

Start

1. Has the member been involved in an incident that could have caused a head injury or concussion, e.g. a fall from a horse?

No

Yes

No action required

Member to be referred to hospital for further assessment. Member must not ride again that day and should be returned to the care of their parents / guardians. Member should not be left

2. Was the rider unconscious at any point?

Yes

No

3. What medical cover do you have onsite?

Doctor or Paramedic (Route A)

Trained or Qualified First Aider, including coaches (Route B)

4a. Has the Doctor / Paramedic confirmed the member has suffered from a head injury or concussion?

Yes

No

Member does not ride again for **three weeks** at any activities and should follow medical instructions given by the medical professional. This may include immediate referral to hospital depending on symptoms.

5a. Has the Doctor / Paramedic diagnosed the member as suffering from a suspected head injury and/or suspected concussion?

No

Yes

No action required

Member to be referred to hospital immediately for a suspected head injury for further assessment. Member must not ride again that day and should be returned to the care of their parents / guardians and should not be left alone.

Member to be assessed by first aider before being allowed to continue

4b. Has the member suffered a confirmed or suspected head injury / concussion?

Yes

Unsure

No

No action required

Refer to a Doctor / Hospital for further assessment. Member must not continue riding until they have been assessed.

6. Has the hospital confirmed the member has suffered from a head injury or concussion?

No

Yes

No action required

Member does not ride again for **three weeks** at any activities and should follow medical instructions given by the medical professional.

7. Do the parents / guardians want the member to ride again before the three week period has passed?

No

Continue as planned - Member does not ride again for **three weeks** and should follow professional medical advice about restarting any contact sport.

Yes

Medical evidence of member's fitness is required before they can ride again. **Note:** This letter must be obtained from a medical professional (Doctor, hospital consultant, etc) and dated at least ten days after the incident where the injury was sustained.

Please note, if you are unsure at any stage, follow the 'yes' route.

APPENDIX H – GUIDE TO ORGANISING THE TACK AND TURNOUT COMPETITION

It is recommended that the Organiser of any Prince Philip Competition understands how to organise a Tack and Turnout Competition – if the tack and turnout takes a long time, the whole day can be disrupted.

We advise Organisers to allocate three Judges and a writer to the tack and turnout section, they can each be given specific job, i.e.

- ▸ Judge 1 can check the pony.
- ▸ Judge 2 can check the tack.
- ▸ Judge 3 can check the rider

The writer helps to make the job for the Judges a little easier.

Please note that all of the Judges should be up to date with the current Tack and Turnout rules and have a rule book to hand.

Before the competition it is advised to create a timetable allocating the time which each team must present to the Tack and Turnout Judges, these timetables can be posted to teams beforehand.

Allow each team approximately 5 minutes to be checked and judged. Additionally, try to allow some additional time before the parade in case there are any issues that need to be referred to the Official Steward.

If a team presents a 6th Member at Tack and Turnout, they are checked but their score is not noted.

FIXTURES FOR 2024

NATIONAL STUDY DAY

- ► 4th February – Bury Farm Equestrian Centre, Mill Road, Slapton, Buckinghamshire, LU7 9BT

TRIALS FOR THE DAKS HOME INTERNATIONAL COMPETITION

- ► Northern Ireland – 24th February – Silverwood Arena.
- ► Wales – 3rd March – Dyffryn Farm, Berriew, Welshpool, SY21 8AE
- ► England – 10th March - Dallas Burston Polo Grounds.
- ► Scotland 10th March - Morris Equestrian Centre.

DAKS HOME INTERNATIONAL COMPETITION

Royal Windsor Horse Show from 1st to 5th May

ZONE FINALS

- ► Southern Zone – 6th July - Southfield House, Somerset, BA11 3JY
      Areas: 10 / 13 / 14 / 15 / 16 / 18
- ► Northern Zone – 6th July – Overton Farm, Crossford, Carluke
      Areas: 1 / 2 / 17 / 19
- ► Central Zone – 20th & 21st July Stanford Hall, Leicestershire.
      Saturday - Areas: 6 / 8 / 9 / 11 / 12
      Sunday - Areas: 3 / 4 / 5 / 7

THE JCB PONY CLUB CHAMPIONSHIPS 2024 - Offchurch Bury, Offchurch, Leamington Spa, Warwickshire, CV33 9AW

- ► Junior Championships - Friday 9th August
- ► Intermediate & Pairs Championships – Saturday 10th August
- ► Senior Runners-Up Competitions – Sunday 11th August

PRINCE PHILIP CUP FINAL - H.O.Y.S.

- ► Horse of The Year Show at Resort World, Birmingham – 9th to 13th October 2024

PREVIOUS WINNERS

- 1957   North West Kent
- 1958   Cheshire Hunt (North)
- 1959   High Peak Hunt
- 1960   High Peak Hunt (North)
- 1961   Enfield Chace Hunt
- 1962   High Peak Hunt (North)
- 1963   Angus
- 1964   Atherstone Hunt
- 1965   Blackmore Vale Hunt
- 1966   Woodland
- 1967   Hurworth Hunt
- 1968   Angus
- 1969   Taunton Vale Hunt
- 1970   Atherstone Hunt
- 1971   Atherstone Hunt
- 1972   Strathblane And District
- 1973   Strathblane And District
- 1974   Kirkintilloch And Campsie
- 1975   Peak
- 1976   Wylye Valley Hunt
- 1977   Banwen And District
- 1978   Eglinton Hunt
- 1979   Cheshire Hunt (North)
- 1980   Oakley Hunt
- 1981   Banwen And District
- 1982   Eglinton Hunt
- 1983   Eglinton Hunt
- 1984   Eglinton Hunt
- 1985   Atherstone Hunt
- 1986   Wylye Valley Hunt
- 1987   Eglinton Hunt
- 1988   Eglinton Hunt
- 1989   Oakley Hunt West
- 1990   North Warwickshire
- 1991   Wylye Valley
- 1992   Eglinton Hunt
- 1993   Eglinton Hunt
- 1994   Eglinton Hunt
- 1995   Eglinton Hunt
- 1996   Eglinton Hunt
- 1997   Oakley Hunt West
- 1998   Clydach

- 1999   Poole & District
- 2000   Eglinton Hunt
- 2001   Oakley Hunt West
- 2002   Oakley Hunt West
- 2003   Wylye Valley
- 2004   West Perthshire
- 2005   Eglinton Hunt
- 2006   Banwell
- 2007   Atherstone Hunt
- 2008   Oakley Hunt West
- 2009   Percy Hunt
- 2010   Devon & Somerset
- 2011   Oakley Hunt West
- 2012   Oakley Hunt West
- 2013   Strathearn
- 2014   Warwickshire Hunt
- 2015   Monmouthshire
- 2016   East Kent Hunt
- 2017   Oakley Hunt West
- 2018   West Hants
- 2019   West Hants
- 2020   -
- 2021   West Hants
- 2022   North Herefordshire
- 2023   North Herefordshire

2024 SPONSORS

With grateful thanks to:

- Hollywood Bowl
- Equestrian Games UK
- PG Sports UK
- STRUK Events

Printed in Great Britain
by Amazon